THE LIBRARY BINDING MANUAL

LIBRARY BINDING MANUAL

*A Handbook of Useful Procedures
for the
Maintenance of Library Volumes*

EDITED BY
MAURICE F. TAUBER

LIBRARY BINDING INSTITUTE
BOSTON, MASSACHUSETTS
1972

QUALITY IS NEVER AN ACCIDENT. IT IS ALWAYS THE RESULT OF INTELLIGENT EFFORT. THERE MUST BE THE WILL TO PRODUCE A SUPERIOR THING.

JOHN RUSKIN

TABLE OF CONTENTS

CHAPTER NINE   63
THE FUTURE OF MAINTENANCE OF
MATERIALS

> MECHANIZED INFORMATION STORAGE AND RETRIEVAL
> SYSTEMS—NEED FOR IMPROVED MATERIALS—PERI-
> ODICALS AND PAPERBACKS.

CHAPTER TEN   67
LIBRARY BINDING INSTITUTE STANDARD FOR
LIBRARY BINDING

APPENDICES   81

FOREWORD

This Manual has been designed as an introduction to binding for libraries. It is intended to assist librarians in the preparation of materials for binding, and to instruct them in the care of their collections. Although more intensive use of this Manual will be made by personnel in public and school libraries, attention is also given to binding problems of college, university and special libraries. Books, periodicals, other serials, pamphlets, newspapers and other printed materials are considered.

This is the third edition of this work and is the first to be issued by the Library Binding Institute. The first two editions were issued by the American Library Association in 1951 and 1952 respectively. It is written in such a way that it can be used by librarians and their assistants on all levels. It is also anticipated that library science school students and others interested in binding will find it useful in their work.

In this revision, there is an effort to bring discussion up to date on such matters as specifications, types of binding, and pre-binding. Binding is treated here for the first time in the Manual as part of the total framework of maintenance of collections.

Those involved in this revision owe much to the second edition, published in 1952, and prepared by Louis N. Feipel and Earl W. Browning. They are also indebted to Dudley A. Weiss, Esquire, Executive Director and General Counsel of the Library Binding Institute, for his suggestions and for making available useful materials and data. The individuals who have assisted in its preparation include Nathalie C. Batts, Hilda Feinberg, Linda M. Kruger, Ralph L. Scott, Edith C. Wise, Richard J. Hyman, Irlene Roemer Stephens, John Veenstra, and Marianne Von Dobeneck. Mr. Hyman and Professor Stephens were especially involved in the revision of the text. Mr. Scott contributed to the enlarged glossary, as well as aiding in other ways in preparing the manuscript for the printer. Mrs. Feinberg prepared the index.

Since it is quite clear that binding and other care of materials are essential for effective library use, it is important for librarians to have a binding policy in order to make full use of funds.

Because the terms "LBI Standard Library Binding" and "Class A" are used interchangeably, both are used in this volume.

Grateful acknowledgement is made to the publishers and authors who gave permission to use materials included in the appendices.

MAURICE F. TAUBER
Melvil Dewey Professor
of Library Service,
Columbia University

PREFACE

The Library Binding Manual was first published about twenty-five years ago. When I suggested to Professor Tauber that it was time for a new edition and offered him access to the LBI files if he wished any data we might have, the only request made was that the volume be not only useful to professional librarians and their staffs but also that it be a teaching tool in schools of library science.

The reasons for this request lie in the fact that the thousands of requests made to LBI over the years for information or help, in matters affecting the maintenance of library volumes, evidence a need for an expanded Library Binding Manual. These requests come from all over the world and, by and large, seek concrete, practical information. There are excellent volumes on conservation practices which relate to the more or less permanent preservation of the physical form of the volume. Library binding and, hence, this volume, is confined to the maintenance of a volume for reader usability and the maximum number of circulations, uses or withdrawals.

We are living in a period in which new and unusual media are being developed and used for the storage and communication of data. This is understandable and necessary as an inevitable result of the proliferation of knowledge in a technical society. It is significant, however, that the greatest expansion in numbers of books and periodicals has taken place concurrent in time with the initiation of mechanical and electronic innovations.

This tremendous and growing inventory of books, coupled with the accelerated growth of libraries to house them, and the emphasis on careful training of librarians as key personnel in the meaningful use of library materials, requires renewed consideration of the efficient and economic maintenance of such materials for the use of library patrons. The purpose of this volume is to assist in this process.

DUDLEY A. WEISS
Executive Director
Library Binding Institute

CHAPTER ONE

SOME BASIC CONSIDERATIONS IN BINDING AND LIBRARY BINDING

HISTORY OF BINDING

Bindings were in use long before printed books. For thousands of years before the codex became our standard book format, our ancestors were placing protective covers on clay tablets and on papyrus and parchment scrolls. Nor was the later handwritten or printed codex left unprotected; the pages of the codex had to be kept in a jar. The purpose of the clay envelope or parchment sheet or wooden board was to preserve the written record for present and future readers. Incidentally, from the very beginning, these covers also served to identify and classify the contents. The Sumerians labeled the clay envelope covering the tablet, the Greeks and Romans attached tags to their scrolls, and today, still, on any book in our libraries, we will find not only the publisher's identification but our library's classification and location codes. (See Appendix 1.)

TODAY'S REASONS FOR BINDING

Bindings were designed to preserve the written record for the reader as well as from him. The modern book must also be protected against exposure to the elements and the deterioration resulting from the passage of time. It must be strengthened, too, against the heavy use which our society's dependence on the printed word has made so necessary. Careless and sometimes malicious handling poses threats to the preservation of the printed word. The protective cover and the way in which the volume is bound may, at least, minimize potential damage and prolong the useful life of the volume. (See Appendix 2.)

OUR COLLECTIVE RESPONSIBILITY

The preservation of cultural and intellectual heritage in printed form is the collective responsibility of many individuals and groups. No one, in good conscience, in or out of the library, who is concerned with books, can avoid this duty. The responsibility for preservation is shared by publishers, suppliers and manufacturers who create the book, the librarians who serve as custodians and interpreters of the printed record, the binders who bind or rebind specifically for library use, the library administrators who must allocate funds for binding, and, especially, the community which uses the books.

THE PROBLEMS OF MODERN PAPER

Binding makes available material for the library patron when and where he wants it, in a usable form and at a proper cost. Up to the middle of the nineteenth century, the printed book, because of its rag content paper, promised durability and longevity. Hazards of vigorous or unfortunate use or of accident were always present, but these were hazards that the quality of the book's material helped minimize. There are thousands of incunabula—books printed in the fifteenth century—the paper of which appears and feels as though it were made yesterday. Today, however, it is recognized that practically all of the books printed after the first half of the nineteenth century are much less durable, since the papermaking process utilized a woodpulp stock. Today's binding, therefore, is designed to prolong the usefulness of library materials in spite of the weakness of the paper.

Several years ago, W. Elmo Reavis, in a discussion of book sewing as distinguished from book stitching, specified that oversewing is necessary because modern book paper must be sewn. Such sewing is moderate in production cost, suitable for a wide range of papers, and has initial strength without straining the paper. Hence, it is appropriate for long and severe service. (See Appendix 3.)

Attention directed toward providing proper book bindings, as well as selecting the library binder who supplies this service, are of basic importance to everyone concerned with library administration.

VARYING REQUIREMENTS FOR LIBRARY BINDING

Binding for the library must always satisfy the different requirements imposed by various kinds of materials and the ways in which the materials will be used inside and outside of the library building. There are books of many sizes and shapes, newspapers, journals, maps, color plates, music and rare books. Some of these materials will be in constant use as reference sources in the library; others will circulate for leisure reading; and still others, because of their value and irreplaceability, will have to be read under supervision in the library.

Binding procedures for the library can never be a mass production routine, automatically applicable in the same way to all types of materials. Judgment, knowledge, and experience must enter the process at every stage. The library binder must be a craftsman with a sure sense of how form must follow function in the preparation of materials for library use. The librarian, similarly, should constantly be cognizant of the range of users and the ways in which certain materials are used. A music score, for example, will be of little use if it cannot be placed for reading on the piano.

FRESH LOOKING VOLUMES

Readers are attracted to the library with volumes which have bright, interesting covers, and pages which are not over-mended, soiled or torn. The library staff, too, is likely to have a more cheerful attitude toward their work if the volumes they handle are fresh and clean.

The desire of every librarian is to have attractive volumes to offer his public. To achieve and maintain this desirable condition is a never-ending struggle. One method used in many libraries is to issue fiction in the publisher's cover as long as its condition will warrant, and then rebind. Present-day fiction and some non-fiction published in paper bindings, however, can become disagreeably soiled after a very few issues unless protected by an extra plastic cover.

Cloth-bound non-fiction volumes can circulate, in most cases, approximately thirty (30) times before they need rebinding. Cloth-bound children's books, like the formerly cloth-bound fiction, can be kept in circulation approximately thirty (30) times without losing their attractive appearance, if they have been properly sewed by their publishers. Once rebound by the LBI Standard, such volumes may be expected to furnish one hundred (100) or more additional circulations or uses.

If a volume is ever to be rebound, the best, most economical time to send it to the bindery is before its appearance becomes so unattractive to readers that its circulation slows up. It should not be allowed to become so hopelessly worn out that it cannot be rebound, but has to be replaced. If the sewing has given way in one or more places, or if leaves are loose, the volume should be rebound, even though the cover can last a few more circulations (provided, of course, that it is of any permanent value to the library).

To keep a volume circulating until it is so crippled that it cannot be put into sound condition except by expenditure of much time in mending, repairing and rebinding is inadvisable. A good binder can do wonders with a bundle of dog-eared, shabby paper. For a book of permanent value, unobtainable in good condition, it may be worthwhile to test his ingenuity; but ordinarily it is not a profitable undertaking. Volumes that need rebinding, emergency mending or treatment, should be brought promptly to the attention of the binding supervisor. This should be the responsibility of every staff member from page to librarian.

PRE-LIBRARY BINDING

A second method is to buy fiction, children's books and so-called "classics" in pre-library binding. These volumes may be expected to furnish one hundred (100) or more circulations. They are bought by the library binder in sheets or in the publisher's binding, and are bound or rebound to the Library Binding Institute Standard for Library Binding (based upon the Standards for Reinforced—Pre-Library Bound—New Books, originally issued by ALA in 1939) before being sold to libraries. While there are many titles available in prebindings, they are generally confined to adult fiction and to children's books and are by no means representative of the variety of books that are ordinarily rebound (when worn out) for permanent library stock. A volume thus bound can be kept in constant circulation without rebinding, until it is ready to be discarded. Most are bound in bright, illustrated covers, and retain their reader appeal until discarded.

Sometimes publishers offer what they term "special" bindings for library use. Some may be good, while others may be little more than the publisher's regular edition. Unless these "prebound", "reinforced", or "reconstructed" books measure up to the Library Binding Institute Standard for Library Binding, their acquisition may be seriously questioned, especially if they are sold at an increased price, where circulation with minimum wear is desired.

A particularly serious situation exists with respect to the

various publishers' editions of children's books. There is no one standard observed by publishers for such volumes, and, hence, the quality of such volumes varies from publisher to publisher. Many represent their volumes as "prebound" or "publishers' library binding", when, in fact, they are trade editions which may or may not have been reinforced. (See Appendix 4.)

The standard for "prebound volumes", referred to in the Glossary of Phase II of "Development of Performance Standards for Binding Used in Libraries", *Library Technology Project, American Library Association,* 1966, Page 19, reads as follows:

> *Prebound—Term applied to new books bound (prior to or at the time of original sale) according to either the ALA "Standards for Reinforced (Pre-Library Bound) New Books" or the "Library Binding Institute Standard for Library Binding".*

SOME COMMENTS ON TERMINOLOGY

The terms binding, rebinding, prebinding, conservation, preservation, Class "A" and other words are used frequently in a generalized rather than specialized way, and this may influence the manner in which library collections are maintained and books are repaired or rebound.

"Library binding" was defined in the first edition of the *Library Binding Manual* (Chicago: ALA, 1951) as "(1) A special form of bookbinding for strength and durability to withstand severe library use. Distinguished from Edition Binding. (2) The process employed in producing such a binding."

In a subsequent printing of the LBI Standard, the first part was changed to read "(1) Volumes bound according to this standard whether rebinding of new or used volumes, prebinding of new volumes (also called prebounds, pre-library bound), and binding of periodicals as distinguished from publishers' edition binding, library edition, or other binding not in accordance with this standard. . . ."

A distinction should be made between "preservation", "restoration", "conservation", and "maintenance of library materials". Books are the packages or containers for information. As such, they are consumable. Library bookbinders seek to conserve the useful life of volumes that ultimately will be expended or replaced. They seek *to maintain the useful life* of the volume by replacing the package. Keepers of rare books seek to *preserve* not only the content but the container so as to pass them on to posterity in the best possible state.

Librarians generally seek to have valuable items *restored* to their original condition.

Where a volume is a rare book and part of a permanent collection, the terms "preservation" or "conservation" might well be used. Such volumes may well be bound other than by the LBI Standard, for they should not be oversewn, since they may have to be rebound more than once. Whether the entire physical collection, or only a few volumes are to be preserved for posterity, as distinguished from the content, techniques must be used which are not covered in this volume. Reference is made to the following full treatments of that technology, both of which have helpful bibliographies:

Cunha, George Daniel Martin: *Conservation of Library Materials; A Manual and Bibliography on the Care, Repair and Restoration of Library Materials.* Metuchen, N.J., Scarecrow Press, 1967.

Horton, Carolyn: *Conservation of Library Materials: Cleaning and Preserving Bindings and Related Materials* (2nd ed., revised), Chicago, 1969, Library Technology Program. American Library Association.

Smith, Richard D.: "New Approaches to Preservation," *Library Quarterly* 40, January 1970, pp. 139-171.

Where a volume is subjected to the rigors of use characteristic of a circulating or reference library, the problem is not one of preserving the publication for posterity, but rather maintaining it for as long a period, and for as many uses, circulations or withdrawals, as possible at the minimum cost per use or circulation. In respect to serials, the element of preservation for research purposes is significant.

The LBI Standard (based on the "Minimum Specifications for 'Class A' Library Binding" issued by the Joint Committee of ALA and LBI) was developed, and is still the primary reference to maintain a volume for such use. Written resources are an essential part of our culture, whether for education, research, vocation or recreation. Replacement of certain items may not even be possible today, and conservation is basic for service.

This volume is concerned primarily with the maintenance of volumes for use, as well as for the preservation of certain types of materials, such as periodicals and other serials for posterity. Hence, when dealing with library binding the phrase "maintenance of materials" is used. In much the same way that in industry provision is made for the replacement of parts in equipment, so in libraries allowances should be made in the budget for administration and personnel costs for the maintenance of collections of books, periodicals, and other material for the convenient use by clientele.

CHAPTER TWO

HOW THE LIBRARY BINDING INDUSTRY AND STANDARDS DEVELOPED

PRIOR TO 1900

Throughout the nineteenth century, binders were taking care of books for libraries which in the earlier years were all privately owned. There was as yet no distinctive library binding or library binding industry concerned with the problem of binding volumes subjected to many circulations. It was evident, however, much before 1900, that books subject to repeated use by groups of readers needed a kind of binding sturdier than that of privately owned and less vigorously handled materials. Only after the turn of the century was a method or technology created for binding and rebinding books with materials and methods specially adapted for libraries.

1900-1924

A pioneer in this special type of binding was Cedric Chivers, who purchased the printed sheets from the publisher and bound them specifically for library use. Chivers emphasized strength of material used in binding, together with sturdy construction. Such library binding was made possible by the development of an efficient oversewing method for manufacturing the book. Chivers established plants in America as well as his native England.

Librarians were soon establishing cooperative arrangements with binders to maintain desirable binding standards. Among the oldest standards in American library science is that for library binding. In 1905, the American Library Association created a Bookbinding Committee "to act in an advisory capacity to membership at large on all matters pertaining to binding, rebinding, magazine and pamphlet binding."*

In 1915, the ALA prepared suggestions for library binding in its Library Handbook, No. 5, entitled "Binding for Libraries."

The first specifications for *library binding* were evolved by a cooperative effort of librarians and library binders working through their respective professional and trade associations. In 1923, a set of general specifications for library and school bookbinding was prepared jointly by the ALA Committee on Bookbinding and the Library Group of the Employing Bookbinders of America. This cooperative body represented the supervisors of binding in large libraries and library binders of acknowledged standing from all over the country.

The librarian chiefly responsible for drafting the specification was Mary E. Wheelock, of the Cleveland Public Library, who worked with Frank M. Barnard of the Employing Bookbinders of America, one of the precursors of the Library Binding Institute. Other distinguished librarians and public-minded library binders who helped in the development of specifications are: Joseph V. Ruzicka, Sr., Elmo Reavis, Oscar Schnabel, Ernest Hertzberg, Lawrence D. Sibert and J. Howard Atkins.

The "General Specifications for Library and School Book Binding" were approved by the ALA Committee on Bookbinding and the Library Group of the Employing Bookbinders of America, and first appeared in *Library Journal* of September 1, 1923.

Thus was instituted the standardizing of methods and materials to meet the requirements of library usage. The purpose of the standards was to make possible a clear understanding between buyer and seller as to what was being bought, thereby eliminating misrepresentation in the sale of library binding, and establishing a basis of fair competition. Reputable binders began to adopt the standards.

1924-1934

Although during this decade there was still more than one method of library binding practiced, binders tended to conform to the specifications. This tendency was strengthened by technological advances. In 1920, a machine for oversewing was perfected by W. Elmo Reavis, and the industry began to be known as the *library binding* industry, as distinguished from

* ALA. Annual Report, 1920-21, p. 29.

other types of binding. The machine had revolutionary impli-
cations for the industry. It reduced the cost of library binding
occasioned by use of hand labor and began the mechanization
of many library binding processes.

As it concentrated more and more on a library-intended
product, one part of the bookbinding industry found its inter-
ests to be different from that of other binders. Hence, a separate section was set up in the Book Manufacturers' Institute
(BMI) when it was formed in 1933. That same year the ALA
and BMI issued "Minimum Specifications for Class 'A' Library Binding."

The ALA Executive Board Minutes for December 27,
1934, contain the following action:

> *VOTED: That the Book Manufacturers' Institute and
> the American Library Association appoint a joint com-
> mittee whose duties shall be to encourage and, if pos-
> sible, insure the widespread acceptance and adoption by
> libraries and binders of the specifications for library bind-
> ing adopted by the ALA Council June 30, and to facili-
> tate discussion and solution of problems of common in-
> terest to binders and libraries.*

By 1934, "library binding" meant binding done by *library
binders* according to specifications. The policy of ALA and
the library binding industry had been clearly stated in the
1934 "Minutes". The next two decades saw this policy implemented.

1934-1954

The library binders' section in the Book Manufacturers' Institute withdrew in 1935 and formed its own separate organization, the Library Binding Institute. A Joint Committee of ALA
and LBI was thereupon created by the Executive Committee
of ALA to have jurisdiction over the specifications. In 1938
and 1952 the Joint Committee amended the Specifications for
Class "A" Library Binding.

In 1939, standards for prebinding, modeled on those for rebinding, were approved by the Council of ALA, LBI, and the
Book Buying Committee of ALA. The official title was "Standards for Reinforced (Pre-Library Bound) New Books, January 1939."

The Joint Committee throughout these two decades followed the mandate of the ALA Council in obtaining "wide-

spread acceptance and adoption by libraries and binders of the specifications for library binding." In 1954, because of legal considerations, the Joint Committee was dissolved by ALA. Within ALA, a Bookbinding Board continued.

1954-TO DATE

So well had the Joint Committee pursued its aims that in 1956 a member of the ALA Bookbinding Committee was able to say:

> *The Minimum Specifications for Class A Library Binding have become the accepted Standard for library binding. By adhering to these standards, inferior binding has largely disappeared from the library scene. It is a sturdy binding, good for hard-used books like the reserve books in a public library. These books may circulate a hundred times a year. Minimum Specifications for Class A Binding is an economical binding for such books.* (Library Trends, *Vol. 4, No. 3, January, 1956, p. 308.*)

Thus, the objective of the ALA Council was achieved. In addition, the future course of an industry was predetermined. In the development of a standard for library binding prior to 1923-1934, there were two schools of thought. One believed that librarians should state what they expected from a volume subject to library use (a "performance" standard). The other believed that a given performance can be assured only when materials and methods of manufacture are precisely specified.

The latter school of thought prevailed in ALA when the "Minimum Specifications for Class 'A' Library Binding" and Prebinding were adopted. Thereafter, the technology and economy of the industry were shaped by the specifications. Equipment was developed by machinery manufacturers, knowing that there were definite processing steps and an assured market for enough machines to warrant development expenses.

The specifications were amended by LBI several times, the most recent revision being in 1971. (See Chapter Ten.) They have had general acceptance. The manufacturing methods have changed and library binderies have become semi-automated with sophisticated equipment for most operating steps, including computers, electronic and hydraulic equipment. Productivity per man hour has increased, with the result that, despite cost increases, prices have increased at a rate substantially less than those for new books and periodicals. (See Appendix 7.)

The Library Binding Institute, recognizing its obligations to the libraries of America, and cognizant of the responsibility imposed upon the library binding industry to maintain the tremendous investment in library volumes for reader usability, adopted many experimental and far-reaching programs, including probably the only In-Plant Quality Control Program adopted by any industry serving libraries. Every Certified Library Binder is visited periodically by an impartial expert and every operation is checked. (See Appendix 8.) Management Practices and Training Programs have been instituted as part of a continuing program of education of management personnel. Procedures have been established for the testing of new equipment and materials. Upon petition of LBI, the Federal Trade Commission has issued "Trade Practice Rules for the Library Binding Industry" which set forth the legal obligations of fair practices as between a binder and his customer and as between competitive binders. (See Appendix 9.)

OTHER STANDARDS—LIBRARY TECHNOLOGY PROGRAM

Although the dominant standard for library binding is the LBI Standard, there are three other book standards, as well as standards for materials used in bookmaking.

The *Official Minimum Manufacturing Standards and Specifications for Textbooks* is a materials and methods specification issued by the National Association of State Textbook Directors, the American Textbook Publishers Institute and the Book Manufacturers' Institute.

Specifications for Lesser Used Materials was issued by ALA June, 1957, and approved by LBI. This is a materials and methods specification for storage materials. It has not had a wide acceptance among libraries, since the requirements of many libraries vary as to this type of material.

Proposed Performance Standards for Binding Used in Libraries was issued in 1966 by the Library Technology Program of the American Library Association. Earlier it was pointed out that before the Class "A" specifications were developed there were two approaches to the problem of a standard for library binding. The one that was adopted by ALA and LBI was a Standard based on materials and methods specifications. This was in the 1930's. Years later, when the Library Technology Project was established, it adopted a policy of developing, whenever possible, performance standards, rather than specifications of materials and methods. This position is based on the theory that, as consumers, the principal concern should not be with how a thing is made (that is the concern of the manufacturer), but how it will perform (which is the only concern of the consumer).

With this as its premise, probably the most comprehensive study yet made of binding problems of libraries was begun, resulting in two publications relating to Performance Standards. To date, no industry group has adopted or approved the proposal, except the Library Binding Institute which has recommended approval of the durability, openability, and general appearance provisions as expressions of what a consumer requires. Inasmuch as the LBI Standard does meet these requirements, it coupled its recommendation with the proposal that ALA should approve the LBI Standard as an expression of the library binding industry's method of satisfying library requirements, and that both should be American National Standards Institute standards. *Publishers' Weekly* (December 11, 1967) expressed the view of book manufacturers and publishers in an editorial written by Daniel Melcher, then President of R. R. Bowker Company, and Leonard Shatzkin, Director of Book Manufacturing, McGraw-Hill.

They stated:

> *"Thus there are now LBI standards for heavy duty library rebindings and pre-bindings, and there are the widely used textbook specs—but nothing for publishers' library editions. . . . Speaking practically, the so-called 'standards' (referring to the proposed performance—ed. note) are not standards at all. They are proposed testing methods. However, they are no less interesting because of this. They represent an earnest effort on the part of librarians to pin down satisfactory performance in a publisher's library binding. How to deliver such performance with adequate quality controls, is the problem of the book industry."*

The LTP study determined, through a survey, librarians' requirements in terms of openability, workmanship, and durability. It tested, both in the laboratory and in the field, various types of volumes, new and rebound, and established a laboratory equivalent for wear by use of a special testing machine (Universal Book Tester).

It appears clear from the study that Class "A" volumes (LBI Standard) met all of the requirements libraries seek in volumes.

Historically, library binding was among the first standards adopted by the library profession. Class "A" specifications have served the library world satisfactorily. What LTP seeks to do is to minimize the librarian as a factor in how volumes are bound. By so doing and by specifying what it seeks by way of performance, it believes that new ways of binding books may be developed.

The library binding industry, through LBI, criticizes this approach, pointing to the fact that the library binding industry was developed on the basis of the ALA approved specifications and did meet the purposes set forth in Phase II* (p. 28) with respect to durability:

> *The basic purpose of the program was to develop standards that would make it possible for a librarian to purchase with some degree of confidence a binding designed to withstand certain specified tests in the laboratory and that might be expected to remain serviceable for a given number of circulations.*

With respect to *workmanship* (p. 32) the proposed standard is a guide and restates substantially what LBI has previously issued.

With respect to *openability,* there is no problem. Volumes that are suitable for oversewing and that are properly oversewn will open within the tolerable ranges. Volumes where the printing is against the grain may be oversewn but hand sewing and stubbing of pages may be required; this is a matter of expense.

The administrative procedures for purchasing library binding, recommended in the Phase II study, provide a method which some large library systems with extensive staffs may find suitable, but it is doubtful that it would be applicable to most libraries. Most libraries have very limited budgets for library binding in terms of the relation of dollars spent to other expenditures. To maintain a collection demands more than merely a specification or standard. A system whereby there is a flow of material from library to binder and back again, together with constant attention by all personnel to the condition of the collection is a necessity. No lot of volumes (100 or more) has the homogeneity necessary for the proposed sampling procedures to be valid. The fact that some

---

* *Development for Performance Standards for Binding Used in Libraries, Phase II* . . . Chicago, American Library Association [c1966] (Library Technology Report, No. 10)

volumes in a shipment test one way is no proof others will follow the same pattern, since most volumes sent to a bindery vary as to dimensions, construction, materials and condition of wear. Testing to destruction is contrary to the actual use of library volumes by clientele.

Book manufacturers point out that volumes bound according to the textbook specifications, and all Smyth-sewn volumes, cannot meet openability tests. They also raise questions as to whom they must satisfy—the publishers for whom they do the manufacturing, or the publishers' customers.

These are only some of the questions raised by the LTP study, and it may be some time before they are resolved. This much, however, is certain: The effect of this study in stimulating thinking on the subject should be recognized.

The Chairman of the Advisory Committee for Development of Performance Standards for the ALA, stated upon their issuance that the Standards were only provisional. "Those responsible for preparing them are fully aware of their limitations. Further research is needed to make the standards complete, and experience in their actual use will demonstrate how they may be improved." (*Publishers' Weekly,* June 12, 1967, p. 77)

Probably of more significance in the long run is the fact that the growth of American libraries in the past decade has resulted in a tremendous growth in collections. The library profession is properly concerned with defining library needs, and the library binding and publishing industries are equally entitled to determine how each shall meet those needs.

As the size of the market for library binding grows, the economics of the situation ultimately will prevail, but a dialogue between the industry and the profession should lead to results beneficial to both. In the meantime, librarians can be assured of meeting their responsibility for maintaining their collections by the use of Class "A" for materials requiring this standard.

CHAPTER THREE

MAINTENANCE OF MATERIALS BEGINS IN THE LIBRARY

ORGANIZATION WITHIN THE LIBRARY

In 1937 Randolph G. Adams startled librarians by describing them as "enemies of books." Insofar as all interested parties within the library and those affiliated with the library (for example, trustees) do not do their best to conserve and maintain the library's materials, this still has point. The maintenance of library materials is an all-library problem because it requires constant surveillance of materials before and during use, and the assurance of proper handling by staff and patron.

It is essential that an over-all program for maintenance be concerned with every piece of material in the library from selection to discard and for twenty-four hours during the day through proper ventilation and housing. Trustees and purchasing agents should be aware of the budgetary needs of binding and realize that this budgetary support must be continuous if arrearages are not to accumulate until unmanageable financial problems arise. Even with liberal binding budgets, there is always the necessity of having to decide which materials are to be chosen. Every item should be maintained in such condition that patrons are satisfied with it. The ultimate test of maintenance of materials is reader usability. This is particularly true of new libraries which are developing their collections. Today, also, with the heavy concentration of periodicals, especially new titles, in libraries, it is essential for librarians to be concerned with completeness of volumes in all details of collation in respect to issues, supplements and indexes.

DEPARTMENTAL COORDINATION

Binding in many libraries is a haphazard operation. In general it is not wise for a department preoccupied with a major responsibility to accept binding as a minor duty.

All departments of the library should be coordinated with the one responsible for binding. The Acquisitions Department can choose, whenever possible, materials which promise to be durable. The Cataloging Department can mark for special treatment materials presenting special conservation problems, if this has not already been signaled by Acquisitions. The Reference Department can advise on which indexes and other bibliographical aids should be included when binding periodicals, and advise on which reference works need special protection because of bulk or heavy use. The Circulation Department must watch patron use of materials and, also, should not shelve or handle books carelessly. Because of its constant use of bindery services, the Periodicals Department can be of constant help to the other departments in the preparation of volumes and in making certain volumes are complete. In short, every person in the library, user or staff member, is in some way concerned with the binding program.

BASIS OF A SOUND BINDING PROGRAM

If a sound binding program is to be established within the library, there must be a set of defined procedures. Assignments of authority and responsibility are essential.

Methods and techniques for maintenance of materials must be determined. Policies on binding, mending, discarding have to be set. Negotiations must be carried on with the bindery. These are some of the duties which must be assigned to those involved with the binding program.

A sound program needs a budget adequate to maintain the collection for the purpose for which it is intended. There is no sense in intricate acquisitions procedures which are not complemented by preservation of the items collated. The budget must, therefore, be planned and implemented on a functional basis.

Class "A" Library Binding should be used for all permanent material to be kept in the form of books and for all material subjected to normal library use.

There are many library binders in the United States. For most purposes, a library should specify Class "A" library binding (LBI Standard). While many library binders can do work meeting these specifications, a library binder who is Certified has demonstrated his capacity to do Class "A" (LBI Standard) work, and warrants his work to be Class "A" (LBI

Standard) unless otherwise noted on his invoice, his warranty being given subject to the Federal Trade Commission Trade Practice Rules for the Library Binding Industry. (See Appendix 10.)

ESTABLISHMENT OF PROCEDURES—LIBRARY BINDING BUDGETS

Responsibility and the necessary authority to discharge it must be assigned to one person in the library who should become familiar with book and paper construction. As part of the basic instruction of a librarian, every person responsible in any way for binding should visit the plant of a library binder in order to learn how a volume is library bound.

Rules and procedures should be in writing and available to all personnel. A binding manual is highly useful to maintaining consistency. (See Marianne von Dobeneck in Bibliography.)

The budget should be adequate to the library's particular requirements. Library binding should be a separate item in the total budget and should be sufficient both to maintain a collection at a high level for reader usability and to obtain the maximum use from library materials.

The National Advisory Commission on Libraries commented on questions relating to the effective use of library funds and in particular to the question, "Are we getting the most benefit for the taxpayer's dollar spent?" as follows:

> *The pitiful incompleteness and tardiness of library statistics, and their lack of comparability, make it impossible to give specific quantitative responses to this series of questions. No one knows precisely, or even with close approximation, what the total present library expenditures of the nation are, or even what the federal contributions to those expenditures are—nor can even approximately reliable specific estimates be made of the costs of remedying the serious deficiencies in library service that we all know exist. (ALA Bulletin, January 1969, page 74.)*

One of the most striking examples of this lack of adequate data on library costs is in the area of the costs of various segments of library service. It is hard to believe that only one-half or less of American libraries know the cost of putting a book on the shelf. (See Question #4, Appendix 7.)

Expenditures for books and other library materials have

about quadrupled during the 60's. (See *Bowker Annual,* 1969, page 27.) This trend may be expected to continue until this category of expense will equal 45 per cent of total library expenses. The stockpile of library materials may be expected to double every eleven or twelve years. With such a tremendous diversion of national wealth into library materials, the normal accounting and cost procedures, routine in the business world, must be applied to libraries. Hence, the importance of an adequate binding budget, rationally arrived at, is an essential part of an overall library budget.

There are few Model Budgets. "Costs of Public Library Services" (see Appendix 10) is a suggested starting point for the development of a sound budget approach, although it is to be hoped that the item "Binding, rebinding, microform" could be separately stated for each category, with an analysis.

A sound budgetary practice with respect to the maintenance of library materials involves, as a minimum, the following:

1. The inclusion of funds for library binding as a separate and distinct expense item.
2. The education of those responsible for fiscal authorizations and expenditures (trustees, purchasing agents, administrators) of the importance of an adequate binding budget.
3. The responsibility for this education must vest in senior professional librarians.
4. In discharging this responsibility such personnel should prepare written guidelines or policy statements.
5. Such policy statements should be based upon
   (a) provision for periodic review of collections with respect to reader appeal and usability of materials;
   (b) criteria for initial hard cover binding of periodicals (usually budgetary provision is made for such binding at the time a periodical or serial is ordered, if it is to be hard cover bound).

CLASSIFICATION AND TREATMENT OF MATERIALS

Few if any libraries have the funds to provide the optimum care for all the materials in their collections. Decisions must constantly be made as to which materials are to be given priority. Hence, the classification of materials must proceed in accordance with function or end-use of materials.

PERMANENT MATERIALS

Definition: Materials which a library considers basic to its collection. Literary or pecuniary value, replaceability, age, accuracy of information may be pertinent criteria, but essential is the importance of a particular volume to a library's collection. The criteria are whether the volume is to be subject to normal library use, is complete, and is a permanent part of a collection for the foreseeable future. Permanent, as used herein, refers to the data in a volume and not to the preservation of the original physical volume itself.

METHODS OF TREATMENT:

1. *Microphotographic process:* For fragile, rare and expensive materials; for archival or other material which is not lent, such as theses, expensive items; for newspapers and generally for material which is either physically such that it cannot be kept indefinitely, too bulky, or so valuable that its loss cannot be risked.
2. *Lamination:* For old material where it is desired to preserve the original.
3. *Fine Binding:* For unique or very valuable material.
4. *Library Binding* (LBI Standard): For all other permanent material which is kept in the form of books subject to normal library use, or which must be complete and available for use. Most permanent materials, both books and periodicals, fall into this category.
5. *Slip Cases:* For old material that cannot be bound because of condition of paper.

TRANSITORY MATERIALS SUBJECT TO NORMAL LIBRARY USE

Definition: All library materials subject to normal library use or where completeness is a factor, which may at some later date be discarded and thus are not a permanent part of a collection.

Treatment: Such materials should be treated as permanent materials and library bound.

Criteria for Classification of This Material: Circulation or loan figures, physical condition of volume, probable demand, number of copies, importance to collection, historical value, scarcity, possibility of replacement.

TRANSITORY MATERIALS NOT SUBJECT TO NORMAL LIBRARY USE

Definition: Materials recognized as not being a permanent part of a collection, which are little used; and completeness is not a factor of importance to a reader.

Treatment: Depends upon purpose of library, physical condition of material and reader requirements. Such materials do not require Class "A" (LBI Standard) library binding, but library binders will either develop a type of binding meeting the library's particular requirements or bind according to Specifications for Lesser-Used Materials (approved by ALA and LBI) if it meets a library's needs.

SPECIAL MATERIALS

Definition: Any undersized, oversized or odd-sized volume, or any volume that requires special handling.

Unusually Heavy Volumes or Volumes Subject to Unusually Hard Wear or Use: Included are indexes, bibliographies, and other reference materials. Class "A" (LBI Standard) Library Binding may be adequate, although a heavier binding (usually sewing on tapes) is used, but good practice indicates developing a binding recommended by a certified library binder based on the library's requirements.

Poorly Constructed Materials: These include material with inadequate inner margins and poor paper. Various methods of treatment are available including use of adhesive binding and stubbing pages.

Paperbacks: The recent expansion in use of paperbacks has focused attention on handling such material. Library binders have been binding such volumes (usually European and other foreign imports) for many years prior to the current expansion. They should be classified as any other material and treated accordingly. Some may be bound according to LBI Standard where end use requires this and it is possible, others may be reinforced by a variety of devices. Some may be sewn, others require adhesives. Based on a library's requirements, a certified library binder can treat such materials satisfactorily.

Music: Library binders sew through the folds for flat opening.

COST PER CIRCULATION OR USE

In reaching a judgment as to whether to rebind, prebind, or discard a volume and buy a new one, costs are all important.

Ultimately, this determination is based on the cost per circulation or use of a volume, assuming a library has decided to retain the work as part of its collection. The following is an illustration of a method of determining cost per circulation or use:

COST PER CIRCULATION OR USE OF A NEW VOLUME

Average cost of hardcover book—1970 (Bowker Annual 1971)	$11.66
Library's cost to acquire (est.) (LBI 1969 Survey)	3.61
Total cost to put volume on shelf	$15.27

Average number of circulations—26.7
Average cost per circulation or use—57 cents

COST PER CIRCULATION OR USE OF
THIS VOLUME REBOUND

Cost of rebinding (8″ Volume) (LBI 1969 Survey)	$ 2.34
Library's cost to send to binder (est.)	1.00
Total cost of rebinding	$ 3.34

Average number of circulations—92.4
Average cost per circulation or use—3.6 cents

Hence, for a total expenditure of $18.61 ($15.27 plus $3.34) a library obtains 119 circulations at an average cost of 15.6 cents per circulation. If the volume were not rebound, but discarded and new volumes purchased to replace it, to obtain 119 circulations would cost $67.95, since it would require 4.45 new volumes to furnish those 119 circulations. Thus, the expenditure of $3.34 for rebinding a volume may save as much as $50.00 for the library. Furthermore, as a result of ever-increasing productivity, binding prices have increased at a far lower rate than the increase of the price of books and periodicals. The average price of "Selected Hard-Cover Books" in 1957 was $5.29 and in 1970 it was $11.66—an increase of 108%. The average price of rebinding an 8-inch volume was $1.81 in 1957 and $2.50 in 1968, or an increase of 38%.*

* This 1968 rebinding price is the most recent available as of this printing. See Appendix 7.

The demonstrated economic efficiency of library bindings is sufficient reason to provide funds for rebinding of a collection at the same time that funds are appropriated for the acquisition of the collection. The situation is comparable to that which prevails with respect to the purchase of a fleet of motor vehicles. When acquired, funds are budgeted for their repair. Dollars spent for rebinding will free dollars for other library purposes, including purchase of books. This is, in short, the economic justification of the library binding industry.

REPRINTS, PAPERBACKS, FACSIMILE REPRODUCTIONS

Whether to order a reprint or a paperback instead of rebinding involves the cost, the projected use of the volume and its expected life. In terms of cost per circulation or use, if a reprint costs $2.50 and averages 25 circulations, its cost is about 10¢ per circulation and, hence, it is less expensive to rebind.

Paperbacks which are not reinforced may be more expensive than rebinding, since assuming a cost of $1.50 and an average circulation of 5, the cost is 30¢ per circulation or use. A reinforced paperback may be less expensive since it may be expected to give many more circulations. Some library binders sell reinforced paperbacks on a guaranteed circulation or life of the volume basis, but few libraries keep a record of circulations, and the cost of record keeping may be more expensive than rebinding or reordering.

Many titles are available only in paperback and these should be pre-library bound before being circulated. Similarly, facsimile reproductions of volumes should be pre-library bound when ordered so that the volume may serve as a permanent part of a collection.

SHOULD A VOLUME BE MENDED?

Mending must be distinguished from repair or rehabilitation of a volume. Mending is indicated if it involves only minor restoration, and trained personnel is available at low cost to do the work. Mending should not be done if it involves replacement with new material (e.g., missing pages), if separation of book from cover is involved, and if the volume is eventually to be rebound. Poor mending or rehabilitation by untrained personnel may make satisfactory rebinding impossible and the end result may be more costly for the library than not mending.

1. *Mending*. Restoration, not involving replacement with any new material or the separation of book from cover. (For example, the mending of a tear in a page or the tipping in of a loose leaf.)

2. *Repairing*. Partial rehabilitation of a worn volume, the amount of work done being less than the minimum involved in rebinding and more than the maximum involved in mending. (For example, the repairing of the cover cloth or restoring loose leaf corners.)

3. *Reinforcing*. Strengthening the structure of a weakened volume, usually by adding material. (For example, the strengthening of a hinge with cloth or the reinforcing of a page by covering it with tissue.)

4. *Recasing*. Replacing the cover on a volume which has come out of its cover or has loosened in its cover, the sewing and cover being still in good condition.

5. *Rebacking*. Attaching a new shelf back on a volume without any other binding.

6. *Re-covering*. The process of making a new cover and of attaching it to the volume.

7. *Re-sewing*. The process of taking the volume out of its cover, removing the old sewing, sewing anew, and replacing in the same cover.

All of these processes may be carried on in the mending or binding department of a library and are incorrectly called mending or repairing.

Good mending and other methods of keeping a worn book in usable condition require training, care, and a proper knowledge of and respect for books. Poor mending and other rehabilitation methods may easily spoil a volume and render its rebinding impossible. A volume may be made unfit for binding through the application of too much glue or paste on the back of the volume inside the cover—a result often of recasing or pasting the volume back into the original cover. Paste or glue that is too thin may run between the leaves so far that it is impossible to separate the leaves without tearing the entire inner margin or destroying some of the print. This same bad result may come from the use of too much paste in tipping in loose leaves.

The use of gummed cloth or transparent adhesive paper for tipping in, for mending tears, or for reinforcing joints inside the body of the volume that is destined to be rebound may also render rebinding difficult and should be avoided. Removing adhesive strips from tears may easily destroy some of the print. Removing gummed strips along the inner margin (if, indeed, they can be removed) weakens the binding edge, often necessitating extra reinforcing. If such gummed strips are not first removed, the leaves, when the volume is being trimmed, rounded or backed, will skid, resulting in an imperfect, unsatisfactory job. (Skidding may also be caused in volumes in which there are a number of highly glazed photographs.)

Early rebinding for volumes of permanent value is always more economical in the long run than is much mending or rehabilitation work. Mending and rehabilitation are only partial jobs, and should be limited to simple operations on volumes that are never to be bound or rebound, whereas rebinding is complete and includes all the end results of mending, repairing, reinforcing and resewing.

WHEN TO REBIND?

Rebinding should occur before a volume is so worn that it loses reader appeal (and circulation), or is so worn that rebinding is impossible.

Check three things: appearance, broken sewing, loose pages.

BINDERY SCHEDULES

Scheduling of shipments to the library binder is extremely important if a library is to have optimum service. These are questions to be considered:

1. When can the volumes best be spared from the library?
2. When is the most convenient time for preparation?
3. When can the binder do the work with the least delay?
4. When will the library be able to pay its binding bills both promptly and conveniently?

With material other than magazines, a little careful study will show that not all material awaiting binding need be sent at the same time. Some volumes, such as popular fiction, will be found to have just passed their peak use and, perhaps, need not be sent at once. Others, e.g., Christmas plays and stories, Lenten reading and special-day material, have only a brief use and could be sent when this use has passed. Reading material in school and college libraries, needed only during one semester, could be sent at the end of that semester. Volumes that are in constant use should be sent as soon as possible. Before making any shipments the librarian should consult the binder to make sure that he can receive and bind the material without undue delay.

Not all of the numerous magazines now received by libraries are worth the expense of binding. The librarian will naturally select those which have "future" value and will get them off to the binder as soon as the demand for them will permit. Delay in binding magazines results in wear, and in loss of material not easily replaced. Magazines on the same or similar subjects should not all be sent to the binder at the same time. In a larger library with duplicate sets, satisfaction to the reader will be assured if one set is kept while others are at the bindery. A schedule covering a year will simplify the work of the library and provide the greatest use for the public.

Convenience, real or imaginary, custom and habit have led many libraries to send the bulk of their binding in the summertime when binderies are flooded with orders from schools and universities. Many libraries—school and college perhaps to a lesser degree than public libraries—could arrange, by giving the matter thoughtful consideration, to send their binding in regular amounts and at regular intervals throughout the year.

By sending material in regular installments, the library is relieved of the heavy load of magazine and book assembling that results from one-or-two-a-year bindery shipments. Frequently scheduled shipments will cut down the time that volumes needed for reference or for issue are out of use, either waiting to be shipped to the bindery, or waiting to be bound after arrival there.

More regular shipments need not mean more routine work. Sometimes the scheduling of orders more frequently during the year can save work. If the method for deciding which volumes are to be rebound and when, as well as for bringing volumes to the attention of the binding supervisor, is properly organized, it may be found there is much less strain on everybody when the work is done throughout the year rather than concentrated in one or two hectic periods.

How the binder can do the binding for a particular library with the least delay can be worked out only by study and experiment. Preferably there should be one or two conferences between the librarian and the binder early in the year. The librarian, having studied the binding records of the library for the past year or two, should be able to estimate the current year's needs. The binder should be able to determine from his previous year's records what is the most favorable time to receive the library's work.

The person in charge of the library's binding should know at all times what funds are available. He should know whether the money will be made available in monthly, quarterly or yearly sums. He should arrange the binding schedule accordingly so that bills will not come due when no money is available. It wastes his time and money if the binder must send statements month after month before receiving payment; it is also a waste of time for the library to receive and check statements each month. Prompt payment of bills allows the binder to pay his bills promptly and makes unnecessary the extra expense of borrowing money at the bank.

A binding schedule geared to the appropriation, with bills submitted when they can be promptly paid by the library, avoids overspending of the binding appropriation. This also prevents a rush to spend a possible balance of binding funds which would be lost if not spent before the end of the fiscal year.

The principle of spreading the binding work over the year may appear to apply only to large libraries, but this is not necessarily the case. A number of medium-sized libraries served by a relatively small bindery may find it very advantageous to schedule the work more evenly. In some cases it may take a year or more to get scheduling procedures going smoothly and evenly. But every librarian and every binder who helps to schedule the binding of even one library is not only helping to provide quicker and more efficient binding service for that library but for all other libraries served by the same bindery.

CHAPTER FOUR

SELECTING A BINDER

WHO SHOULD SELECT THE BINDER?

In the area of maintenance of materials the responsibility of the professional librarian involves

(1) The criteria for analyzing materials to be rebound, discarded, etc.
(2) The organizational structure for maintenance of materials.
(3) The standards for binding or maintaining materials.
(4) The selection of a binder.

The administrative technician (purchasing agent, etc.) must work within limitations and guidelines set by the professional librarian.

Where, by law, competitive bidding is required, the professional librarian should select those who are eligible to bid. This should not be done until and unless an inspection is made of the facilities of the binder, so that those responsible for letting the bids may be assured that the bidders have the capability of performing any contract that is executed.

By the same token, the professional librarian must establish the specifications for the binding to be done. It is his responsibility to maintain a collection for reader usability and, hence, he must establish the basis upon which such responsibility is discharged. To do so, he must have the requisite authority, for responsibility and authority are opposite sides of the same coin. Purchasing agents and administrators are valuable adjuncts to a library staff within their area of competence. But they must rely upon the professional assistance and direction of the librarian both as to standards to be followed and eligible bidders.

The relationship of library binder and library is quite unlike that of the relationship of all other vendors to libraries. In many respects a library bindery is an adjunct to the facilities of a library. A library binder performs a service, rather than a sale of a commodity. This service is essential to the effective functioning of the library. Most library binders today will furnish four weeks service for most library materials, but all will accelerate this as to specific items upon the request of the library. Hence, it is important for the librarian to select a library binder with whom he is compatible. Where financial arrangements are negotiated, which most librarians prefer, rather than bid, the problems of competitive bidding involving establishing new relationships, record keeping, etc. are avoided.

In selecting a bindery, whether by a negotiated contract, or by participating in a bid, a librarian must determine the binder's capability and responsibility. The prospective binder must as a prerequisite be able to produce Class "A" (LBI Standard Binding).

Certified Library Binders meet this requirement and, in addition, are periodically examined under a Quality Control Program, warrant their work is Class "A" (LBI Standard) unless otherwise noted on their invoice, carry insurance adequate for their customers' requirements, and have subscribed to the F.T.C. Trade Practice Rules for the Library Binding Industry. In selecting a binder, librarians should require, for their own protection, the same commitments from their binders even though they may not be Certified.

WHAT KINDS OF BINDERIES ARE THERE?

There are many kinds of binders, and although they may not involve libraries, every librarian should know what they do and who they are.

1. *Edition binderies* in which books are bound in quantity for publishers and are not intended for the library market. Practically all books purchased by libraries are bound in edition binderies and have to be rebound after relatively few circulations. Publishers' library editions are reinforced editions.

2. *Trade binders* in which work is not done for the customer directly, but for a printer, or for any other binder in the "trade." In general, the trade binder's shop supplements that of the local printer and takes care of work the latter is not equipped to do, such as wire stitching, ruling billheads, making

pads, and similar tasks entirely unrelated to library binding.

3. *General job binderies* in which odd jobs of binding either for the customer directly or for the trade are performed. These binderies may do some edition and some library binding when they have specially equipped and staffed departments.

4. *Pamphlet binderies* in which newly printed sheets of pamphlets or magazines are stitched (with thread or wire) in large quantities for publishers.

5. *Blankbook binderies* in which ledgers and other book-keeping and accounting volumes are bound.

6. *Library Binders.* A Library Binder is a member of the graphic arts industry who specializes in a certain type of binding, but may, and frequently does, offer other services. The Library Binding Institute surveyed its members and reported that many offered one or more of the following services:

Library Binding (according to LBI Standard) (Class "A")
Prebinding (according to LBI Standard) (Class "A")

Textbooks	Bibles
Edition Binding	Fine Binding
Storage Binding	Binding of Music
Paperbacks (hard) binding	Law Books
Blank Books	Newspapers
Rare Books	Theses

Many types of special work as requested by customers

A recent industry survey set forth the pattern of sales by type of library and by type of materials bound. The distribution of sales by type of library was:

Kind of Library	Per Cent Industry Average of Sales
Public Libraries	13.0
Schools (Elem., Jr. & High)	15.0
Junior Colleges	7.0
Colleges and Universities	50.0
Federal Government	4.0
Industrial	4.5
Hospital	4.5
Church	.5
Other	1.5
	100.0%

This distribution of sales is quite different from a study prepared some years ago when public libraries accounted for nearly 50% of industry sales.

Although library binders work on many kinds of volumes, about 60% are periodicals and the balance monographs, paperbacks, reference, etc. The trend towards the initial hardcover binding of periodicals has accelerated in recent years.

The library binding industry is a separate and distinct segment of the graphic arts industry, using equipment which is quite different from the book manufacturing industry and materials substantially more durable. (See Chapter VII.) The reason for this lies in the fact that a library binder must be able to process volumes of varying degrees of wear, dimensions and materials, whereas other binders (other than fine or rare books binders) process volumes, large quantities of which have the identical physical characteristics. Furthermore, to bind a volume properly for library use requires not only building in strength but also inspection to assure completeness. Periodicals, for example, must be collated, i.e., examined page by page, to be certain they are complete (with all issues, inlays, maps, etc.) otherwise they could be incomplete and therefore not meet the test of reader usability.

LIBRARY BINDING INSTITUTE AND CERTIFIED LIBRARY BINDERS

Library Binding Institute is a national trade association whose membership consists of commercial library binders who are Certified Library Binders, their suppliers, and institutional library binders.

The issuance of the LBI Standard (Class "A") is one of the basic programs of LBI. To implement the Standards, Library Binding Institute—

1. Has established a *Certification System* to inform librarians which binders can do work in accordance with the Standards, are reputable, have been recommended by librarians, and carry insurance to protect their customers' property.
2. Maintains a Free Examination Service for librarians to determine whether binding has been done in accordance with contractual requirements.
3. Sponsored the promulgation by the Federal Trade Commission of Trade Practice Rules to insure the highest possible standards of equitable and fair dealing

in the industry and to protect librarians against deceit
and misrepresentations.
4. Maintains a continuous program of research and education involving binders, their customers and suppliers.
5. Has established the use of a warranty on invoices of
Certified Library Binders, stating that work complies
with the LBI Standard for Library Binding unless
otherwise stated thereon. This warranty reads as follows:

WARRANTY

We warrant that the binding covered by this invoice
is LIBRARY BINDING and complies with all requirements of the LBI Standard for Library Binding
except as noted on this invoice. This statement is
made pursuant to Section 2.2 of the LBI Standard
for Library Binding and Rules 1(c) and 4 of the
Trade Practice Rules for the Library Binding Industry, promulgated by the Federal Trade Commission August 20, 1954.

6. Established a Quality Control Program whereby the
plant of each Certified Library Binder is periodically
examined for adherence to a carefully planned quality
control program.
7. Every Certified Library Binder carries insurance to
protect a library's property as follows:

CERTIFICATE OF INSURANCE

"As a condition of our Library Binding Institute Certification as a CERTIFIED LIBRARY BINDER,
we agree to maintain insurance on customers' property in our custody as follows:

1. The insurance contract shall provide for "all-
risk" coverage.
2. The limit of liability for any volume lost or destroyed shall be a sum equivalent to five (5)
times the selling price of the binding for such
volume.
3. The maximum value of any single volume shall
be Twenty-Five Dollars ($25.00).
4. Where a customer places a value on any single
volume in excess of Twenty-Five Dollars

($25.00), it shall be the responsibility of the customer to notify the Certified Library Binder, in writing, stating the value and the amount of insurance coverage desired, and he shall thereupon obtain the coverage as requested."

CERTIFICATION PLAN FOR BINDERIES

Librarians will do well to visit the bindery doing their work in order to acquaint themselves with its personnel and equipment. A binder does not have to be Certified to be able to produce Class "A" work, but the Library Binding Institute has established its Certification Plan for binderies as part of an overall program to maintain high standards for the binding industry. Any reputable commercial binder may apply for membership in LBI for his bindery as a Certified Library Binder, and it will be certified if it meets the following requirements:

1. Samples submitted prove that he can do Class "A" (Library Binding Institute Standard) work. (These samples are examined by a Panel of Examiners or a Quality Control Coordinator.)
2. Satisfactory library and financial references as to reliability are furnished.
3. Adequate insurance as defined by LBI is carried.
4. The plant is examined by an LBI Quality Control Coordinator.

It is to the advantage of the library to establish a friendly business relationship with a reliable bindery. Time and money will be saved by such an arrangement. By applying to the Library Binding Institute, aid may be had in selecting a competent and reliable bindery, working out service procedures, and maintaining strict standards. When a satisfactory relationship has been established, the librarian will quite naturally inspect the work done and see that it adheres to specifications, but volumes may always be submitted to LBI for examination.

The librarian should make sure that the bindery soliciting his business, although not a Certified Library Binder, measures up to the following minimum requirements:

1. It is capable of producing Class "A" (LBI Standard binding) with respect to materials, workmanship, and reader usability.
2. It is able to furnish dependable service, retaining books at the bindery only for a period consistent with

producing good work, but also that it have the ability to do a "rush" job when it is a matter of importance, and with mistakes kept to a minimum.

3. It presents a minimum of demands on the library staff in the preparation of books to be bound; and has the ability to follow rules which have been agreed upon by binder and librarian.

4. It takes the best possible care in handling library materials and carries reasonable insurance protection adequate to protect library volumes in its custody.

5. It furnishes a warranty of quality under the Trade Practice Rules for the Library Binding Industry.

6. It maintains an in-plant quality control system.

TO BID OR NOT TO BID

Most library binding in the United States is sold on a negotiated basis, and a continuing relationship persists between the library and the library binder. In many cases the bindery becomes for many purposes an adjunct to the library facility, so close is the relationship in maintaining the collection at par.

Where a bidding is required for library binding, the following are sound rules:

1. The professional librarian should select those binders to whom invitations to bid are issued and such selection should be made on the basis of the prospective bidder's productive capacity and technical ability to fulfill the contract.

2. All terms in the bid should be specific. Where Class "A" (LBI Standard) Library Binding is specified, an appropriate clause may read as follows and if inserted obviates the necessity of spelling out all the specifications, whether it be for new or worn volumes, periodicals, rebinds or prebinds.

   All volumes included in this contract shall be bound to conform in every particular to the Library Binding Institute Standard for Library Binding (Class "A") and the vendor shall so warrant on his invoice.

3. Specify that the vendor affix a warranty on his invoice in the same form as on page 52.

4. Do not include meaningless terms. For example, if your library requires 30 days or more to process bills

for payment, a discount for payment prior to 30 days
may be meaningless, if compliance by you to take advantage of the discount is not possible. All that such
a requirement does is distort the real price.

5. Furnish all bidders accurate information as to quantities, sizes and other characteristics so that a bid re-
lates in a real way to the work to be done.

6. Specification Compliance: In the event that the Library Director shall so desire, he may submit any
volume as to which there is a question of conformity
to the LBI Standard, or other specifications, to an
LBI Panel of Examiners for a determination of conformity to such Standard. Binding samples, if so requested, shall also be handled in like manner.

A study entitled "Purchasing Library Materials in Public
and School Libraries" by Evelyn Hensel and Peter W. Veillette
(ALA, Chicago, 1969) examines purchasing procedures and
the relationships between libraries, purchasing agents and dealers. This study, prepared for the American Library Association
and the National League of Cities, contains various "Recommendations and Guiding Principles". By and large, it is a fair
conclusion that library materials may well be exempt from
the normal bid requirement of purchasing agencies. Bidding
for library materials is the exception rather than the rule and
of 789 libraries who responded to the authors' questionnaire,
only 15% require bidding for books. While we have no corresponding figure for binding, LBI informal surveys indicate
5% or less of library binding is on competitive bid.

The authors cite the New Jersey Statute (New Jersey Laws,
statutes, etc.), *Revised Statutes* (Trenton 1968 40.33-8.1)
which permit county, regional and municipal public libraries
to purchase many materials, including binding or rebinding,
without advertising for bids. This statute was passed through
the efforts of the New Jersey Library Association, and may
well be a precedent for other states to follow with respect to
binding, not only for public libraries and schools, but also
college and university libraries.

CONSEQUENCES OF USE OF LBI STANDARD FOR LIBRARY BINDING (CLASS "A")

The use of the LBI Standard (Class "A") has had several important consequences over the years:

1. It has provided librarians with an effective budget-saving device. LBI standard binding will assure the maximum circulation or use per volume, thus producing the lowest cost per circulation or use. A recent survey indicated that many public libraries obtained in excess of 150 circulations per volume in volumes so bound.
2. For the librarian, trustee and purchasing agent, the LBI Standard defines the minimum requirements for library binding, so that both buyer and seller have a clear understanding of what is being sold, eliminating confusion and misunderstanding.
3. It has provided a foundation for the development of a specialized segment of the graphic arts industry, for which special equipment and machinery can be economically manufactured. In addition, it has encouraged vigorous competition among library binders based upon quality and service.
4. Standards were designed with the reader in mind—to furnish a complete, readable volume which can withstand repeated use.

CHAPTER FIVE

HOW TO PREPARE MATERIALS FOR THE BINDERY: PART I: SOME BASIC RECOMMENDATIONS

SCOPE

The following recommendations reflect what is good procedural or administrative practice in the handling of binding by libraries. They cover seven areas where uniformity of practice is desirable.

I. Delivery, shipping and invoicing instructions for the library and the library binder to provide economical and quick handling of volumes.

II. The preparation of books in the library for the library binder.

III. The preparation of periodicals in the library for the library binder.

IV. General binding instructions for books sent to the library binder.

V. General binding instructions for periodicals sent to the library binder.

VI. Some recommended uniform practices when binding periodicals.

VII. Non-standard binding.

A library should prepare binding instructions or a manual for its staff and for its binder. A binder should not deviate from instructions unless this is necessary to process the volume, but all deviations resulting in increased costs should be avoided unless absolutely imperative.

I. DELIVERY, SHIPPING AND INVOICE PRACTICES

GENERAL PRACTICE

1. The library and library binder should establish a regular schedule for shipment to the bindery. This schedule should, insofar as is possible, provide for work to be done on a regular basis over a twelve-month period and it should be worked out with the binder.
2. The library should return pickup cards to the bindery promptly.
3. The library should pack all volumes and have them available for shipment even in absence of library personnel or during hours the library is not open to the public. Pack all volumes carefully so that loose leaves will not fall out. Valuable volumes should be so marked, particularly those to be specially insured. Tie all periodicals together by series.
4. The library should separate and pack the work to be processed in different cartons, each carton containing only like material, clearly marked as to contents.
   a. Separate ordinary circulation volumes from reference, rare, and special materials.
   b. Separate volumes according to treatment they are to receive; i.e., separate all LBI Standard Library Binding, fine binding, substandard binding, items to be separately invoiced, personal orders, rare books, etc.
   c. Keep sets together. Remove foreign articles, such as paper clips and bookmarks.
   d. Discuss materials requiring special treatment with your library binder.
5. The library should notify the binder directly of RUSH items, and indicate the date desired, in addition to enclosing the usual list in the carton.
6. The library should, wherever possible, use the binder's invoice system.

II. PREPARATION OF BOOK VOLUMES BY THE LIBRARY

In preparing book volumes for the bindery, the library should follow these practices:

1. Provide binder with total number of items in shipment.
2. Underscore or mark lightly but clearly titles and au-

thors, editors, pseudonyms, or other significant identification, on title page.

3. Include binder's slip for specific colors, transliterations,
abbreviations of too-long titles, lettering of foreign
titles, call numbers, and special instructions on deviations from standard binding. *Exception:* Call numbers
can be legibly written on back of title pages.

4. Tie sets together or otherwise indicate sets that are to
have identical bindings.

5. Send sample volumes or rubbings if matching is necessary.

6. List important reference volumes.

7. Have ownership identification also on other than covers or fly leaves.

III. PREPARATION OF PERIODICALS BY THE LIBRARY

GENERAL RULES

Certain general rules apply to all periodicals:

1. Preparation begins when the serial is ordered.

2. Do not send volumes with missing issues. Your library
binder will advise you where to obtain missing issues.

3. Determine what is to be bound (ads, etc.).

4. Determine whether a bulky periodical is to be bound
in one or more volumes.

5. Specify "Publishers' Arrangement" for placing of index, title page, etc.

6. Specify Standardized Lettering (see Recommended
Uniform Practices for Periodicals, VI below).

SPECIFIC PRACTICES

In preparing periodicals for the bindery, the library should follow these practices:

1. It should keep a binding record for periodicals containing the following information:
   a. How and when published (what constitutes a volume)
   b. If index is published (where and when)
   c. Binding instructions (collating, color, lettering)
   d. Date sent to binder and returned to library

2. Tie together as they are to be bound, i.e., single volumes, two volumes together, divided volumes; or indicate on master slip manner in which the issues are to be bound if different from published volume form.
3. List all titles and number of volumes of each title.
4. Put removable binders' slips of recommended form in each volume under first cover with edge extended, or secured with tying cord. Do not use staples or paper clips.
5. Information on binder's slip:
    a. Check collating and other instruction symbols.
    b. Type or write legibly lettering to be used.
    c. Type or write legibly any special instructions.
    d. Check if new and note color preference.
    e. Check if binding other than library binding.

IV. GENERAL BINDING INSTRUCTIONS FOR BOOKS

The library should prepare and file with the library binder general binding or standing instructions for books covering the following:

1. Preferred colors, use of illustrated or decorated covers, style of lettering, position of call numbers (conflict with printed decorations and design), matching sets, stampings.
2. Instructions regarding volumes with missing pages.
3. Instructions regarding volumes with extraordinary work, e.g., guarding, handsewing, excessive mending, etc.
4. Standing instructions should give the binder discretion to depart from instructions if processing requires it to produce a properly bound volume.

V. GENERAL BINDING INSTRUCTIONS FOR PERIODICALS

The library should prepare and file with the library binder general binding instructions for periodicals covering the following:

1. Collating:
    a. Placement of indexes and supplements
    b. Treatment of covers, advertisements, and extra-textual materials, e.g., book reviews, letters to the editor, etc.

    c. Treatment of publishing freaks, e.g., indexes beginning on verso of title page or contents pages

    d. Treatment and placement of large maps and charts

    e. Substitution for lack of title page

    f. Division of too thick volumes

    g. Use of colored sheets for dividers (in multiple volumes bound together, separation of index from extra-textual materials, etc.)

    h. Missing issues, missing or mutilated pages (return, report, order or stub)

    i. Maps and other matter in pockets

2. Binding:

    a. Color preferences on new bindings or substitutions for discontinued colors

    b. Size changes (if format does not permit old size or ordinary trim)

    c. Handsewing when necessary

    d. Extra work when necessary

3. Lettering:

    a. Supply pattern or rubbings if record not on file at bindery

    b. Preference of lettering on divided volumes (parts or page numbers)

    c. Abbreviations where necessary

    d. Lengthwise lettering where necessary

    e. Standard or regular lettering

    f. Imprints

    g. Call numbers

VI. RECOMMENDED UNIFORM PRACTICES FOR PERIODICALS

1. Title Page, Table of Contents and Index

    a. Bind title page and table of contents at front of volume, index at end.

    b. When no title page is supplied, bind without.

      (1) Alternative—bind first cover.

    c. When index starts on same page with table of contents, bind at front of volume.

      (1) Alternative—when index starts on back of title page, place entire index at front of volume.

      (2) Alternative—bind title page and index at back and stub for title page or bind front cover for title page.

    d. Return volumes with missing indexes to library.
       (1) Alternative—stub for missing indexes and bind.
       (2) Alternative—hold for missing indexes and report.
       (3) Don't bind without index or with numbers missing.
       (4) Effort should be made to obtain microtext copies.
       (5) Cite listings where microtext copies can be acquired.

2. Covers
    a. Remove all covers.
    b. Bind front covers with each issue if each issue paged separately.
    c. Bind back cover in place only when it contains continuation of table of contents from front cover.
       (1) Alternative—bind all covers in place.

3. Advertising
    a. Remove all advertising pages not containing subject matter unless such pages are numbered with text.
       (1) Alternative—all ads out regardless of break in pagination.
    b. Bind in place Editorials, Readers' Say, letters, short articles, etc., although not numbered with subject matter.
       (1) Alternative—remove when not numbered with subject matter.
    c. When advertising pages are numbered separately and contain such materials as mentioned in Section b, retain all advertising pages.
       (1) Alternative—remove all ads regardless of break in pagination.
    d. Bind all ads in place.

4. Supplements
    a. When a supplement (or supplements) is issued separately and is numbered Part 2 of an issue and is paged continuously with the volume, bind in place.
    b. When a supplement (or supplements) is issued separately and is numbered Part 2 of an issue and is paged separately, bind at end of volume after the index separated by a colored leaf.

    c. When a supplement (or supplements) is issued separately and is *not* numbered Part 2 of an issue and is paged separately, bind at end of volume after the index separated by a colored leaf.

    d. When a supplement (or supplements) is included in an issue but is paged separately, bind at end of volume after the index separated by a colored leaf.

    e. When Proceedings and other special features are published in each issue and are paged separately, accumulate at end of volume after index separated by a colored leaf. If such parts have a separate index, bind at end of section.

    f. Spine should be marked to show that supplement is included with basic volume.

5. Missing Pages and Mutilated Parts

    a. If it is found that pages or parts of pages are missing, return volume unbound to library.

       (1) Alternative—report.

       (2) Alternative—supply.

    b. If volume is mutilated, mend what can be done in the usual time required on an average volume, otherwise return unbound.

6. When two or more volumes are bound together, separate volumes with a colored leaf.

7. If a single volume is bound in two parts, bind title page and table of contents at front of Part 1, index at end of Part 2.

8. When any text must be bound behind the index at the end of a volume, insert a colored leaf after the last page of the index.

9. Lettering can be lettered up or down, but desirable that the practice be consistent within each library.

    a. All lettering is to be standard unless otherwise indicated.

       (1) Alternative—all lettering is to be according to previous records. If not, use standard.

    b. If volume is too thin to be lettered horizontally on spine, letter vertically to read down.

       (1) Alternative—to read up.

10. Use library imprint

    a. Alternative—do not use library imprint.

11. Margins

    a. All volumes should be trimmed. If for any reason you find it inadvisable to do so, use best judgment.

b. If journals are of uneven size, make even at top, except when smaller issues are substantially thicker and heavier, jog to bottom to reduce strain on binding.

VII. NON-STANDARD BINDING

The library should furnish the binder instructions for binding of all work not conforming to LBI Standard Library Binding. This includes extra bindings, where specific instructions should be given for materials, repairs, restoration and the like. It includes substandard or storage binding of books or periodicals which are little used (usually such volumes are collated at library, are bound in one color, no special treatment such as hand sewing, and no lettering).

SPECIAL PROBLEMS OF JUVENILES

There are no specifications or standards to which publishers of juveniles uniformly adhere. Publishers individually determine their own specifications and hence, the quality may vary as between publishers. This is confusing to purchasers, but, if the lack of a common recognized standard creates confusion, the absence of a common terminology creates chaos. Terms are used which in effect label the volumes "publishers' library bindings." In fact they are not library bindings but library editions, i.e. "A binding which the publishers feel is adequate for library use." (*The Bookman's Glossary,* 4th Edition, Bowker 1961.)

Most publishers will sell sheets to prelibrary binders who then bind in Class "A", but sometimes this is not done.

The problem here is twofold: First, a determination by the library of the kind of binding it wants to meet its pattern of use, and, secondly, knowing whether what it buys will provide that use. Many publishers' reinforced editions are suitable for library use, but many are not. A prelibrary bound (Class "A") volume will always meet the library requirements. Until there is some easy and efficient way to determine which type of binding on volumes will meet its needs, a purchaser of juveniles should specify LBI Standard (Class "A") and insist on the warranty.

The LBI Standard (Class "A") includes in it the specifications of the "Standard for Reinforced (Pre-Library Bound) New Books" (Jan. 1939) approved by the Council of American Library Association, the Library Binding Institute, and the Book Buying Committee of American Library Association.

CHAPTER SIX

HOW TO PREPARE MATERIALS FOR THE BINDERY: PART II: SOME SPECIAL POINTS

"STANDING" INSTRUCTIONS

Thanks to the LBI Standard and to the more complete understanding between librarian and binder, few volumes, except magazines, sent to the bindery by public and school libraries require any but "standing" instructions. A typical statement of such general instructions might read:

"Except where otherwise indicated by individual binding slips, rebind our books according to the Library Binding Institute Standard for Library Binding in full buckram of assorted colors, letter as per underlined words on title page and find call numbers on title page. We desire author below title and in relatively large type. Use "decorated" and "illustrated" covers as far as possible. On thin books lettering on the spine is to read from head to tail. Edges are to be left plain." This can be modified or adapted as desired.

Once such instructions have been issued to a binder they become one of his records and are to be observed until countermanded. A new librarian (or binding supervisor) should check with the library's binder to find out what binding instructions are in force for that particular library so that there may be complete and mutual understanding.

Some binders would prefer that call numbers, if used, be pencilled lightly, plainly and correctly, as near the center of the title page, or the page following, as possible. Using either of these pages for the call number, rather than the back of the title page, makes the call number more easily and quickly found by the binder.

USE OF BINDING SLIPS

If call numbers are to be used, librarians should specify in their "standing" instructions, or on binding slips, the distance that the *top* of the number should be from the bottom of the spine.

The binding slip if used (and it should be used whenever special instructions are needed for a particular volume) may be either a printed form or a blank strip of paper. The simplest printed binding slip should provide spaces for (1) style; (2) color; (3) lettering; and (4) special instructions.

If a binder prefers to have the binding slip pasted in, it should be attached with a mere dot of paste to the first page following the title page, in a diagonal position with its top toward the inner margin, but so placed that the slip will not be out when the edges of the book are trimmed nor caught by the stitches of the new sewing along the inner margin. If the binder objects to having the binding slip pasted in, it should be placed in the book at the title page and it should protrude.

PACKING AND SHIPPING

Before volumes are packed they should be examined to make sure that each is complete. While the LBI Standard requires that all volumes be collated carefully at the bindery, collation of all volumes of any particular value should be done at the library since no one but the possessor of a book is, strictly speaking, in a position to say whether a particular copy of a particular book is complete or not. The additional collation done by the binder before the volume is taken apart is principally for his own protection, although it does serve as an added check on the completeness of the material as submitted by the library. As the book is being collated at the library it should be made certain that library identification marks are still in the volume, that torn pages are mended and soiled ones cleaned, if possible. If pages are missing, typed or photostat substitutes should be provided by the library or a binding slip should be made out stating "bind as is" or "bind with parts missing." Occasionally the librarian may want a volume bound with stubs to which he hopes in time to attach missing leaves or parts.

Book pockets and cards (if used by the library) should be removed and the volumes and cards or pockets separately counted. If the count tallies, the cards or pockets are filed by author or title in binding tray, and charged out to the binder.

Different circulation systems may require other types of record keeping. Books should not be disturbed once they have been counted.

Before a shipment is sent to the bindery, the binder should be notified of the impending shipment, the number of books included, the number of containers, and the method of transportation.

If it is the first shipment to this binder, the notification letter should also contain "standing" instructions as to the style of binding, materials, color of cloth, the rendering of invoices and similar contract provisions. If, when volumes are sent to the bindery, a formal order from a purchasing department is required, see that such an order goes forward at once. Otherwise the volumes may lie untouched at the bindery awaiting the order. For technical and university libraries which send much unusual material, a list by author and title may serve as a record of what is at the bindery. A carbon copy of such lists should be sent to the binder.

Shipments should be sent at regular intervals and must be carefully packed. Most binders will provide boxes or cartons of a convenient size for shipping binding material. Librarians will, of course, confine their use of a particular binder's shipping containers to shipments to that binder, and will return all unused containers to their respective owners "transportation collect."

When the binder is to pay transportation on a binding shipment, it is to be expected that the librarian will follow the explicit instructions of the binder as to the most inexpensive method of shipment. Shipments by express or even by parcel post are generally too expensive to be considered.

Small shipments should be avoided whenever possible. Volumes should be packed as compactly as possible with enough crumpled newspapers to fill in any space remaining between volumes and the sides or top of container. It is not wise to remove covers from the volume. The saving in transportation charges effected is more than offset by the fact that such shipments never pack well, volumes shift about and volumes become crumpled at the edges.

RETAINING ORIGINAL COVERS

Librarians sometimes stipulate to binders that the original covers be used in rebinding, because they wish to preserve the original appearance of the book or because they think it will make the rebinding less expensive. Original covers, however, should only be saved in the case of rare or valuable books, important first editions, or local imprints. Keeping the old cover with the book as it progresses through the bindery calls for extra time and attention and usually an extra charge.

VOLUMES RETURNED UNBOUND

When volumes are returned from the bindery they should be checked against the book cards or pockets to verify the correct return of all volumes sent to the bindery. In counting the number of volumes returned from the bindery, those returned unbound are sometimes overlooked. The reason for their return in this condition will be found noted by the binder on a slip accompanying each volume. Any of three major causes may have been the reason for not rebinding: (1) The volume may be incomplete. (2) The physical condition of the paper may make rebinding almost, if not quite, impossible. (3) Unusual or extra binding processes may be required that will occasion extra charge above the usual rate. If it is still desired that the volume be rebound, instructions to "bind as is" can be written on the binding slip and volume can be sent with the next shipment to the bindery.

PREPARING JOURNALS AND SERIALS

The problem of caring for, preserving and binding magazines or journals and serials is much more complicated than that presented by the average fiction or nonfiction volume. This job, however, can be simplified greatly by the use of record cards which may be obtained from library supply houses. These cards should be made to carry all the information needed to prepare files for binding. (See previous chapter.) With this information readily available, getting magazines' off to the binder requires little additional information beyond dates and volume number.

When a magazine is included in a shipment to the binder for the first time, the binder should, of course, be given full information concerning it. "Standing" instructions can be issued and make the work of the librarian very simple. For example: "Unless otherwise noted bind magazines according to Library Binding Institute Standard for Library Binding in full buckram to match samples and use standardized lettering. Include indexes, supplements and maps, but discard covers and leaves wholly devoted to advertising. Bind index and title page at front of volume. Trim volume as little as possible and maintain uniformity in sets; leave edges plain."

While it may be possible for the library which binds few but the most popular magazines to issue "standing" instructions to the binder, many misunderstandings are apt to arise and much guesswork on the part of the binder will be necessary unless binding slips are sent with volumes needing special attention. For example, a librarian may state that the pagination of a volume should never be broken, and then complain if supplementary material of different pagination is bound together at the back of the volume instead of with the months with which it was published. Or exception may be taken to the inclusion of pages of straight advertising, in spite of the fact that the removal of the pages would break the pagination. Librarians are urged not to remove pages of advertising but to instruct the binder whether to remove or retain them.

If "standing" instructions have not been adopted, a binding slip bearing the name of the library should accompany each volume. This slip should be placed, not pasted on the first page of the text or, if the index is to be bound in front, then on the first page of the index. If the publisher's index is not easily available, and if the magazine is included in the *Readers' Guide* or other reliable compilation, the individual index to a bound volume becomes of less value, and is probably not worth the effort frequently necessary to obtain or retain it.

If two volumes are to be bound as one, they should be tied together, and instructions—as for example, "Vol. 7-8 1949" —should be entered on the binding slip. Incomplete volumes should not be sent to the bindery with instructions to secure missing parts. The librarian has access to all markets from which to obtain missing numbers, indexes and title pages. If the binder is given this job, which he does not want and is little equipped to undertake, the librarian should expect to compensate him for his trouble.

The volume numbering may not always be suitable for the desirable thickness of a bound volume. The librarian should avoid, if at all possible, the binding of a journal which would be thicker than three inches.

RUB-OFFS

If a rub-off is necessary to match volumes previously bound, follow these instructions: (1) Be sure the lower edge of the thin rub-off paper is flush with the bottom of the bound volume. (2) Indicate the top of the volume with a horizontal line.

(3) Hold paper firmly while you make the rub. (4) Rub pencil (soft lead is preferable) until every letter of each word is clearly transferred. Lines, numbers and any symbols should also be transferred. (5) Designate cover material and color to be used. (6) Designate gold or color of foil to be used in stamping. It should be borne in mind in designating the color of the cover material that the colors will change with exposure to light and that two runs of cloth presumably of the same shade do not always match perfectly.

STANDARDIZED LETTERING

The standardized lettering plan greatly improves the appearance of a library's bound magazines, saves the time of the librarian and eliminates the need for rub-offs for the titles included. The job of keeping a rub-off file at the bindery is difficult and expensive. Reference to the accompanying illustration shows the ease of reading title, volume number, year and months when brought into uniform alignment. The magazines are grouped according to height in five classes lettered B to F. Imprints are placed at the bottom, and all decorative lines and ornaments are omitted. The abbreviation "Vol." is not used; and if the date is within the calendar year, only the date without the months is used. Where the inclusive months run over into another year, two lines are used, as for example: "November-May" (line 1), "1948-1949" (line 2). The H. W. Wilson Company indexes and the Library of Congress catalog cards may confidently be used as acceptable form of magazine titles.

Forethought on the part of the librarian will obviate many of the annoyances with respect to binding magazines. If the publisher sends title page and index on request only, they should be claimed at the proper time. Take the title page and index out of the number in which they are received and put them away in a safe place against the time when the volume is to be sent to the binder. (Use of these by a reader may be allowed, on request, and then the material should go back to its safe file.) And, of course, be sure the title page and index are included when the volumes are shipped off to the binder. If they are missing the binder might be instructed to put in stubs for future insertion.

When a shipment of magazines is sent to the binder, danger of misunderstanding will be avoided if a typewritten list in duplicate is made of the titles, one copy being kept and the other forwarded to the binder.

PRESERVATION OF NEWSPAPERS

Since the day when wood pulp began generally to be used for newspapers, the life of the newspaper became limited. Files of newspapers of a hundred years ago are crisp and usable even today, while newspapers only ten or even five years old are turning brown, and their edges are beginning to crumble. For local history reasons, libraries often seek to preserve their local newspapers, and publishers, upon request, are usually willing to supply an extra subscription without charge when assured that it is to be used exclusively for binding. Much is to be said, from every point of view, in favor of newspapers preserved on film, and most libraries of any size are now using film copies, if at all possible to do so. However, the Association of Research Libraries in its report by Gordon Williams on "The Preservation of Deteriorating Books" (see *Library Journal* for Jan. 1 and Jan. 15, 1966) has warned that archival durability of negative microfilms cannot yet be assumed.

Newspapers which must be preserved but whose condition renders them unfit for binding or filming (and of which film copies cannot be purchased) may have their life prolonged by having their pages covered with some protective material such as chiffon, tissue or acetate cellulose. This protective process is expensive and should be fully discussed with a competent binder before being undertaken. Improvements in microfilming equipment may soon make this unnecessary.

If it is decided to bind newspapers, certain rules, strictly followed, will add to their life. In the first place, no copy of a paper that is to go into a bound volume should ever be put into the hands of a reader, unless in emergency and, then, under strict supervision only. Immediately the day's paper is received, a copy should be examined to see that it is complete and that it is legibly printed throughout. If imperfect, a perfect copy should be procured at once. Local newspaper publishers are often willing to share the expense of having their papers bound or having them reproduced on film.

For storing while the necessary issues to form a volume are being accumulated, each issue should be opened to full page size (as it will be bound). If any of the leaves have not been properly folded, they should be refolded. Loose leaves, if any, should be laid close in to the line of fold. The copy should then be laid flat "as is" (in a box, if possible), and succeeding issues should be added until the necessary number for a volume has been accumulated.

For practical use, newspaper volumes should not exceed approximately 2 inches in thickness "between covers." Volumes of this size are much more convenient to handle, and their binding will withstand strain much longer than when made thicker. Where volumes cannot logically be arranged in the 2 inch size, volumes up to 3½ inches in thickness are practicable. Librarians should issue special instructions with such volumes and should ask their binder for estimates on binding them.

Since readers inquire for newspapers by their dates, they should be bound without reference to the volume numbers given them by their publishers. Lettering on the volume should show the publication name and the inclusive dates bound together. The binder should be instructed whether the volume is to stand on a shelf or lie flat, so that he may arrange the lettering accordingly. If the volume is to lie flat, the lettering should be placed lengthwise along the spine, reading from head to tail.

"Standing" instructions as to binding newspapers can be issued, as: "Except where otherwise indicated by individual binding slips, bind all newspapers according to Library Binding Institute Standard, with edges sprinkled, cover three-quarter-bound, lettering in gold on leather label, reading down the back from head to tail." Such instructions can be varied, as the librarian may wish, to indicate stained edges or edges left plain, covers to be full-bound or half-bound, and lettering to be done in ink or foil, with or without leather label. If "standing" instructions are not issued, a binding slip should accompany each volume. A magazine record card for each newspaper should be kept, on which should be shown which volumes have been sent and when. (Different circulation systems may require other types of records.)

The packing of newspapers for shipping to the bindery should be carefully done in order to prevent any possible crumpling or other damage. The papers should, of course, lie flat in the container.

Because of the perishable nature of newsprint, even in well-bound volumes, and because of the awkwardness in handling these heavy volumes, more and more libraries, as earlier noted, are preserving their newspapers by having them reproduced on film. Even though this is done, certain libraries, where much research is done and where local advertising and local history are deemed important, have found it necessary to retain bound volumes, even after they have been filmed.

CHAPTER SEVEN

HOW A VOLUME IS LIBRARY BOUND

Because the rigid specifications of the Library Binding Institute demand that books and periodicals be bound to a set of standards, the processes adhered to by Certified Library Binders, and the materials used, are all substantially the same. The Quality Control Coordinator, in his rounds of inspection, merely makes certain that minimum standards are met. It is true that binding does vary, even among Certified Binders, but to maintain certification, a binder cannot go below these standards, thereby assuring that even the minimum will produce a book of substantial usage. Most library binders, because of the pride they take in their work, and because they have a heritage of highest craftsmanship, produce bindings which exceed in quality the requirements of the LBI Standard.

Most library binderies are similar in layout because the flow of work is determined by the order in which the various processes must be completed. Whether a bindery is mechanized or hand-oriented, therefore, makes very little difference in the end result. A small number of library binderies can be classed in the category of large businesses. However, most of them are fairly small operations. With few exceptions, their proprietors are men who have inherited skills from their forefathers and started at the bench themselves. Many of them still work side by side with their employees, and on the whole, employees recognize a close community of interest with their employers.

MACHINE WORK VS. HANDWORK

It may be thought, because in few branches of industry has the transition from pure handcraft to mechanization been so marked as in that of bookbinding, that the binder would no

longer be a skilled artisan, and that he has been relegated to
the position of a machine operator. There is no justification for
such an assumption because, no matter how far machines have
been developed, it is the operator's skill which still determines
the end product. In fact, the newer machinery, while exact in
its operation, requires considerable experience and a degree of
understanding which can be acquired only by knowing how a
book must be bound to properly meet the specifications. There
still remains a large and distinct class of workers who depend
on the skill of their hands to perform their specialized jobs and
who merely use machines as tools which are faster in order to
meet today's production demands. In practically all library
binderies, there are those who make equal use of both the
machine and the bench.

THE STEPS IN PRODUCING A LIBRARY
BOUND VOLUME

Essentially, the steps in binding a volume have not changed
much over the years. The changeover from hand-sewing to
machine sewing, which took place back in the early twenties,
probably was the one major development which started library
binding on a new approach. All other developments which
turned the handcraft into a production industry appear to
have resolved around the sewing process since this constituted
a difficult bottleneck to overcome.

The invention of one machine, of course, gives birth to
others as can be seen in the picture story which follows. The
pictures shown have been taken in a cross section of binderies
around the United States so that a typical bindery might be
created which will be representative of all Certified binderies.

PRE-LIBRARY BINDING (PREBOUND
LIBRARY BOOKS)

Some Library Binders do what is known as PREBINDING.
This term applies to the binding of NEW books in order to
provide an original volume which is far more durable and far
more economical than the publisher's edition binding or so-
called publishers' library editions. The binding operations are
similar to those used for rebinding except that in many cases
the prebinder may purchase unbound, gathered and folded
sheets directly from the publisher so that he won't have to go
through the stages of removing covers, sanding backs, etc. The
prebinder also purchases illustrated covers in quantity and

PRODUCING A
LIBRARY BOUND VOLUME

A pictorial review of the
Library Binding process

*Old, battered and torn books are received from the library or
school for rebinding. They are unpacked, counted and given a
number to identify the lot with the library or school to which it
belongs. All material is carefully checked and recorded.*

*Periodicals, when received from the library, should be tied in vol-
umes with title page, index, and all issues complete. Instructions
should specify whether or not advertising sections should be removed.*

Each book is carefully checked and recorded. If it is a standard title, or one which the bindery has previously bound, the rub-off or cover lettering is taken from the file so that the type for the cover may be set in the proper style and with the proper spacing.

Old books must be taken apart—the covers thrown away. At this time, tears are carefully mended with Japanese tissue, light weight bond paper or perma-film. This is part of the COLLATING process which makes certain that no pages are missing and that all are in proper order. This is a very important step in library binding. If pages are missing, the book is returned to the library for instructions or disposal.

Collating of magazines and periodicals involves the removal of wire staples—sometimes as many as a hundred in a single volume. Issues must be in proper order, and if the advertising sections are to be removed, careful attention must be given to see that all the material is complete.

The backs of books are carefully sanded on a special machine to remove old glue and lining material and to separate the folded sections into single sheets. This must be accomplished with the least possible loss of back margin because if the back margin is too narrow, it will make the book difficult to read. Some publishers, in the interest of economy, and to save paper, make their back margins too narrow and this is a constant problem for the library binder.

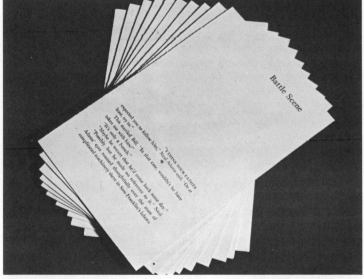

After sanding, the book must be made ready for sewing. However, before this is done, it must be lightly glued to hold it together and then be divided into sections from about fifty to sixty thousandths of an inch in thickness. This should be done on a device specially designed for this purpose, but skilled operators can accomplish this by hand with amazing tolerance. In this machine a set of stepped knives sections the book in one motion. Following this operation binders score each section to make the book easier to open when the condition of the paper indicates this procedure is appropriate.

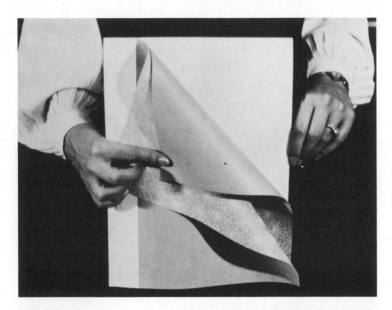

The book is now ready for its end papers. End papers are what hold a book in its cover. They consist of three functional parts: a pasted down or outward end leaf, which becomes the cover lining, at least two free fly leaves, and reinforcing fabric. They are specially made of extremely strong stock and must meet the standards of quality set by the Library Binding Institute.

The strength inherent in library binding is found in its sewing. There are essentially three forms of sewing. The oldest method, of course, is hand-sewing which is done on a frame, and is still done on books which are too large to be sewn by machine. Hand-sewing uses the oversewing stitch and is done by women of long experience.

Thin books are generally Singer-sewn, that is they are sewn through the edge much in the same manner, and with the same type of stitch used in dress-making. Music and narrow margin books are fold sewn.

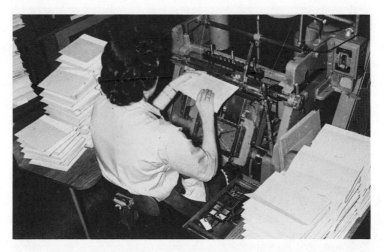

Oversewing is probably the most interesting process involved in library binding. The Oversewing Machine was invented about fifty years ago and is essentially the same as it was then because no improvement in the result has been discovered. Here the sections are pasted and sewn together with the end papers. Each section is sewn in consecutive order so that any single section is sewn to no less than three other sections to provide incomparable strength.

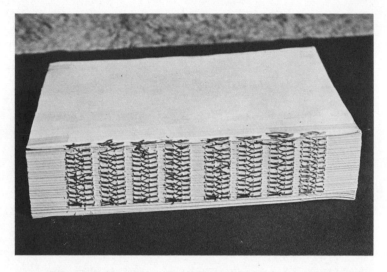

This close-up picture shows what a book looks like when oversewing is completed. It is practically impossible to pull this book apart by hand.

Following the sewing process, the books are trimmed top, bottom and front. At this point, it is actually a book without a cover—its end pages are in place and the pages are permanently held together. Rounding and backing is a term used to describe the process of making a book convex in back—concave in front, a shape all good books should have to provide easy reading and good looks. For years this process was done by hand—a truly back-breaking process. Now modern machinery does it quickly and efficiently.

Backing shapes a ridge on each side of the back of the book. This compensates for the thickness of the cover board and provides a hinge line for the swing of the cover.

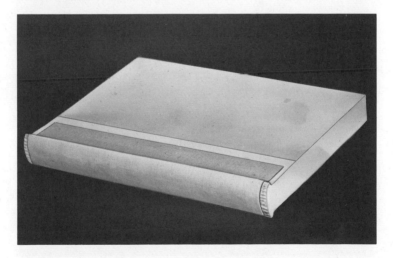

The book is now ready for its back lining which is a strip of approved material extending nearly to the top and bottom of the spine of the book and about an inch and a half beyond the back on either side. A special adhesive is used for the back lining and it must lie smooth and flat without any bubbles in its surface. The back lining not only helps to preserve the shape of the back but serves to hinge the volume.

The boards which will form the covers are now selected and fitted to the book. These boards are made from very special "binders' board" material made to standards approved by the Library Binding Institute. They should not be confused with chip-board or paste-board which could never be strong enough for this purpose.

Cover material, which is made of "Library Buckram" is stocked in three ways: precut to popular sizes, in rolls for cutting to individual size, and in pre-printed illustrated covers which follow the appearance of the publisher's original dust jackets. Such covers are available for most popular juvenile titles and are cataloged for ease of ordering.

The cover of a book consisting of its glued boards and fabrics, is called its case. This picture shows the boards being positioned on the glued fabric in a case gauge which has been designed for this purpose.

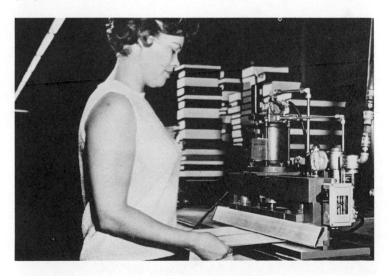

Next comes the turning-in process which means turning the edges of the cloth over the outer edges of the boards. This must be done with extreme care. The machine, shown here, has been developed specifically for this job, is faster and more efficient than previous hand methods.

The corners are also made at the same time the turning-in is done. There are two styles of corners which are acceptable in library binding.

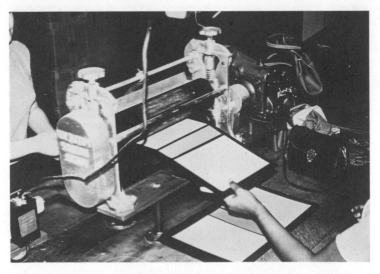

After the edges have been turned-in, the covers are run through a press which looks like a wringer. This smoothes wrinkles and rough places which may be in the cloth and also removes all the air bubbles.

Covers which are not pre-printed with pictures, titles or designs require stamping of the title, author, etc. on their spines, and sometimes on the front of the covers. This is often done in gold or colored foil on a hot press. However, first the type must be set, and this is done on a linotype or other typesetting machine which casts slugs of type.

To properly position the type on the cover, it is marked to rub-off. It is the rub-off that makes it possible to standardize the lettering on books and magazines of the same title.

Although hand-stamping still is being used in some instances, automatic equipment speeds up the work and produces an even, perfectly positioned impression. In the rebinding of books, automation is impossible since each book has a different title and each title is positioned in a different place.

Now the cover is complete, the book is complete, and they are both ready to be assembled into a finished volume. This can be done by hand or by machine. Extra large volumes, magazines and newspapers still have to be done by hand. Such an operation requires skill and strength. Basically, the process consists of pasting the end papers to the inside of the cover.

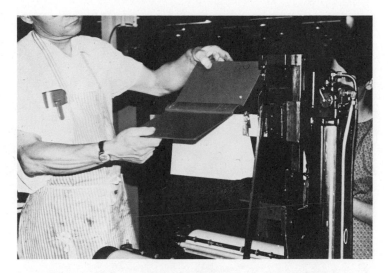

Automatic machinery is now available for casing-in regular volumes. This machine is fast and efficient because it adjusts for any size or thickness of book, centers the cover and in one up and down cycle of the wing, completes the process.

Not long ago, the finished book had to be put in a hand press for twenty-four hours, to dry out flat. Today, a modern hydraulic machine such as this accomplishes the same result in a few seconds. This machine not only presses and dries the book, but assures a perfect hinge for opening and closing the volume.

Finished library bound books are clean, crisp and ready for many more circulations. Each is thoroughly inspected prior to shipment.

Here the books are waiting to be packed and shipped back to the customer. Even the packing materials are of heavy duty quality.

gears his production to quantities of a single volume rather than to the rebinding of one book. The prebinder is also a wholesaler who stocks thousands of popular titles, mostly juvenile because these are ones which may be expected to receive the greatest wear and abuse.

CHAPTER EIGHT

HOW TO EXAMINE BINDING:
A TEN POINT CHECK LIST

Books and periodicals are consumable commodities. The primary function of library binding is to extend for reader usability the life of a volume which, being part of a collection, is subject to use and abuse.

A librarian wishing to determine whether a volume meets the LBI Standard may utilize LBI's Free Examination Service, simply by sending the volume to the LBI office where an examination will be made by an expert with a high degree of competence in the maintenance of library materials. A detailed, written report will be sent to the librarian and the volume returned to the library.

It is possible, however, for a librarian to make a cursory check of a volume to determine whether it appears to meet requirements without reference to an expert. However, if in doubt, the volume should be examined by an expert.

Use of this simple check list should be routine in the library when volumes are returned from a binder.

GENERAL APPEARANCE

1. Examine a book closed—back, sides, top and bottom —for general appearance.
   a. Does cover fit at the back? It should not be too tight or too loose.
   b. Is cover the proper size for the book? It should not project so far beyond the body of the book as to appear oversize nor be cut so close to the book itself as to give an overtrimmed appearance.
   c. Is cover free from signs of excessive warping?
   d. Are joints (grooves) straight and neat?
   e. Are boards of the proper thickness for the book?
   f. Are edges trimmed neatly?

2. Examine lettering.
    a. Is it legible?
    b. Is it properly planned, centered, and arranged?
    c. Is it straight?
    d. Is it deeply and uniformly impressed? Uneven impression may not be noticed at the library until months later, when its separate letters become indistinct or disappear.
    e. Is waterproofing over the lettering of a clear material, lightly applied and so evenly spread as to be practically unnoticeable?

INTERIOR WORKMANSHIP

3. Open cover (front and back).
    a. Are joints flexible (not too stiff)?
    b. Are boards cut neatly and uniformly?
4. Examine each cover.
    a. Is cloth of proper "weight"?
    b. Is cloth cut precisely? (Cut edges will show under the paste-down of the end papers.)
    c. Is turn-in ample?
    d. Are corners neat?
    e. Is adhesion of cloth to board adequate at all points?
5. Examine end papers.
    a. Are they of strong paper, of neutral color?
    b. Are they neatly cut and properly pasted?
    c. Are they properly constructed? All end papers should consist of three parts: (1) a pasted-down or outward end leaf, which should be firmly and evenly pasted down, to become the cover lining; (2) at least two free fly-leaves; and (3) reinforcing fabric.
6. Turn to title page.
    a. Have title and instructions, if any, been accurately followed in the lettering on spine of book?
7. Lay the volume flat on a table and beginning at first and last sections slowly and carefully open and press down a few pages at a time, progressing toward the middle of the volume.
    a. Does book open satisfactorily, considering the nature of the paper and the fact that the book is newly rebound?
    b. Are margins adequate? Where possible, a wide

center margin is more important today to make photocopying possible—especially in the case of periodicals.

c. Where paper is moderately stiff, are sections scored?

8. Raise the closed volume, slowly open the covers all the way back and fan out the pages from the middle, so that sections separate themselves naturally (if machine-sewed).

   a. Are sections uniform and of just the right thickness? (Not thicker than twenty sections to the inch in the case of ordinary paper—slightly thicker in the case of flexible pulpy paper.)
   b. Is back flexible?

9. Examine sewing.

   a. Is book tightly sewed?
   b. Does it open flexibly?
   c. Are the sections of proper thickness?
   d. Are the stitches along the inner margins a uniform distance apart and done in a neat manner?

10. Have instructions to bindery been followed completely and carefully? Were special instructions followed concerning the color and material to be used, or the handling of maps or plates in a volume? Has the binder affixed on the invoice, unless otherwise noted, his warranty that the binding is LBI Standard?

Careful inspection and examination should not be confined to just one or two volumes in each lot returned from the bindery, but should be given to as many books as possible, and by different staff members. It will be found very much worthwhile if at least one person in each department and branch library is taught how to examine bindings and is given the opportunity to examine those received.

If it is found that the binding conforms to specifications at each step in this examination, the librarian may be reasonably sure that the volume adheres to the LBI Standard for Library Binding.

Of course, a complete examination of the sewing, gluing and backing cannot be made without dissecting the volume. This is not desirable unless there is serious doubt that Standard binding has been furnished; as indicated earlier, it is possible to submit the volume to LBI's Free Examination Service.

LATER EXAMINATION

Bindings should be examined not only when they are received fresh from the bindery, but also when the rebound book is worn out and is to be discarded. Then it can be determined whether or not the library has received its money's worth. Such an examination will show that it is not the first cost of rebinding that is of most importance but that it is the number of issues and the number of years the book has given service that really count.

With the poor grade of paper used in many books being published today, and with their narrow margins, too much cannot be expected even if the books have been bound by the best binders. If a book is found that has cracked open in the middle, examine it closely before blaming the binder. The paper, too porous to hold stitches any length of time, may be to blame, or the binding margins may have been so narrow that the book could not be rebound to open easily and some impatient reader may have forcibly broken its back.

Every volume is thoroughly inspected before it leaves the bindery, but binderies, like libraries, cannot always maintain staffs with the desirable amount of training and experience. Mistakes will sometimes creep in. When found, the volumes having mistakes should be returned to the binder without delay; mistakes are not too readily rectified or adjusted after a lapse of considerable time. If no mistakes or imperfections in binding are found, a word of appreciation from the librarian would encourage the binder and his staff to increase their efforts to give their best possible service.

CHAPTER NINE

THE FUTURE OF MAINTENANCE OF MATERIALS

MECHANIZED INFORMATION STORAGE AND RETRIEVAL SYSTEMS

The extraordinary growth in this country since World War II of the student population, information resources, research needs of government and industry has resulted for all libraries in severe problems of bibliographic control. Not only must libraries keep up with the flood of publications, they are expected to control and distribute for their patrons the information in those works. There has been much discussion on automating information systems on a national basis, using computers to classify, store and retrieve information, converting our book resources into microforms or computer memory, doing away with the card catalog, providing information via television screen at an individual console from a central store of knowledge.

Most of this is still discussion. Some experiments are in progress, but there is yet no indication that our present libraries, particularly school, public, and college, will be able to dispense with books—and their maintenance problems—in the foreseeable future. There are many reasons for this. First, mechanized storage and retrieval systems are most needed for non-book materials used in specialized, scientific research. The research scientist searching for information in technical journals and reports is engaged in a kind of reading totally different from that of the public or college library patron who is finding his way to the writings of Hawthorne or Hemingway. Thus, the kind of material most subject to computerization is very unlike the basic book stocks of most public and college libraries.

Interestingly enough, one of the few successful examples of

mechanized bibliographic control in public libraries, that is, the production of computerized catalogs in book form, shows that binding is still needed to make the book catalogs themselves available for their intended public use. Undoubtedly, the production of book catalogs will increase during the next decade.

A second major reason for the survival of books into the foreseeable future is that the book format affords the most comfortable and convenient means for reading and studying, particularly of any extensive nature. The 1964 report, *Automation and the Library of Congress,* prepared at the request of the Library of Congress, makes numerous suggestions for mechanizing bibliographic control, but affirms that the book as such may be expected to continue as an important information medium.

Most scholars and librarians are frank to admit how much less convenient and pleasant it is to have to use microform copies of printed matter. Of course, microfilm and microform are often unavoidable if we are to preserve the contents of deteriorating paper and if we are limited, like almost all libraries, in storage space. Nevertheless, microforms are not as easy to use as books and, for the public library patron or college student, browsing is made almost impossible.

Books, therefore, can be expected to survive along with microforms and possible mechanized information storage and information systems. After all, neither the motion picture, sound recording, radio, nor television has been able to displace the book as a medium of communication. Nor has the popularity of automobiles, spectator sports, and television viewing succeeded in destroying books' recreational appeal.

What, then, are some of the current problems in maintenance of materials we must face?

NEED FOR IMPROVED MATERIALS

Any librarian who has ever seen the floor of the stacks area strewn with brownish flakes need not be reminded of the problems resulting from the deteriorating wood pulp paper, extensively used in this country since the 1870's. Much research has been done, under the auspices of the Council on Library Resources, Inc., by the late William J. Barrow who decided that the principal cause of such deterioration is the paper's acidic quality. He developed a formula for non-acidic permanent/durable paper which he claims may for all practical purposes be considered of permanent durability. His hope was that publishers will make use of his formula so that books may prove longer lasting. He also recommended deacidification and lamination for deteriorating paper items which must be preserved in original form. Another of his research discoveries is that low temperatures prolong the life of paper, so that books might in the future be put in "cold storage" for archival preservation.

The development of permanent/durable paper would be all the more welcome since we have no scientific proof at present that microfilm copies are permanently durable. This is not to deny the value of microfilm, but only to state a necessary caution which future research will hopefully render unwarranted.

PERIODICALS AND PAPERBACKS

The last two decades have seen a phenomenal increase in the publication of periodicals and paperbacks, particularly the "quality" paperbacks. Both journals and paperbacks present serious maintenance problems.

The *Standard Periodical Directory* 1970 (Oxbridge Publishing Company, Inc. N. Y.) lists 53,133 publications, weighs nine pounds and totals 1,550 pages.

As more and more periodicals and journals are made available and have to be acquired, libraries become more and more cramped for storage space and more puzzled as to how these materials may best be preserved. In many cases, microfilm or microform is, as already noted, highly desirable. Many microform editions are now available which can either be the only subscription for journal and newspaper or be used as the reference copy after the original has been discarded. We must remember, though, that materials are thus made less easily accessible under certain conditions and that microform reproduction of color printing is still relatively new and quite expensive. Also, microfilm or microform reading machines are required. These machines take up considerable space and usually must be placed away from the main reading areas whose lighting needs are different. It is usually more convenient, too, for the machines to be near where the microforms are kept.

There will always be some journals and magazines which the library, particularly the public library, will wish bound in their original form. Binding problems of serials will, therefore, still be with us and they will probably become more complicated as more periodicals change their names, dimensions, and numbering systems. The suggestions given in Chapters Five and Six on preparing materials for the bindery should be carefully noted. The most important point is to be aware of the problems, to reach *some* decision on them, and to have the resultant instructions in written form available for the librarians and the binder. For example, agreement on standardized lettering would considerably simplify the work of both library and bindery—and also help the reader. In the initial hardcover binding of periodicals, it is recommended that titles be stamped on the spine following the *Recommended Practice for Use of CODEN for Periodical Title Abbreviations* (ASTM E250-70).

Paperbacks are now available for many important titles not procurable in hard cover editions. Such items should be bound in accordance with LBI Standard if the quality of materials in the paperbacks' construction makes this at all possible. Some quality paperbacks now have sewn rather than adhesive bindings.

The quality of the so-called "perfect" binding (single leaves held together by adhesive) has improved considerably since its first use in mass-distributed paperbacks. Barrow investigated the durability of adhesives and claims a quality to be attainable which would make such adhesives practically permanent. A series of reports on his investigations of adhesives and other book materials has been issued by the Council on Library Resources, Inc.

Perfect binding is not part of the LBI Standard. If future developments justify, after the most careful investigation, that such a process could be used to advantage at least in some of the binding operations, the Library Binding Institute would consider incorporating the process in its Standard. Until then, it is recommended that library binding for paperbacks be done only in accordance with LBI Standard, when the volume is to be subjected to the same usage as other library volumes requiring Class "A" binding.

CHAPTER TEN

LIBRARY BINDING INSTITUTE STANDARD FOR LIBRARY BINDING

(Revised)

Issued by Library Binding Institute, 1971

1. PURPOSE

The purpose of this Standard is to specify materials and manufacturing processes for LIBRARY BINDING. It is intended to apply to the rebinding of new or old volumes, the binding of magazines and periodicals, and the prebinding of volumes for library use.

This Standard represents the best judgment of Certified Library Binders of the minimum specifications necessary to produce a volume which will achieve two objectives: first—meet the requirements of libraries for an end product capable of withstanding the rigors of normal library circulation or use, and second—provide maximum reader usability. It is the latest revision in the specifications for LIBRARY BINDING, the first of which were issued in 1923.

Only binding, including rebinding, prebinding and periodical binding, in accordance with this Standard is LIBRARY BINDING, but nothing in this Standard excludes other types of binding, whether superior or inferior to LIBRARY BINDING, for library use, as determined by a librarian and his Certified Library Binder for any specific purpose.

2. SCOPE

2.1 *Definition.*—This Standard covers the library binding of three general classifications of volumes: (1) ordinary book-volumes, (2) ordinary periodical volumes, and (3) special volumes. It specifies materials to be used, the manufacturing processes and definitions.

2.2 *Warranty Label.*—To assure the purchaser that the binding being sold is library binding complying with all requirements of this Standard, each seller shall include the following statement, or its equivalent, in conjunction with his name and address on labels, invoices and other written material representing the binding to be library binding:

WARRANTY

We warrant that the binding covered by this invoice is LIBRARY BINDING and complies with all requirements of the LBI Standard for Library Binding, except as noted on this invoice. This statement is made pursuant to section 2.2 of The LBI Standard for Library Binding and Rules 1(c) and 4 of The Trade Practice Rules for the Library Binding Industry, promulgated by the Federal Trade Commission, August 20, 1954.

3. CLASSIFICATION OF VOLUMES

3.1 *Ordinary book-volume.*—Any ordinary-sized graphic material consisting of an appreciable number of leaves or folded sheets produced originally as a unit and submitted for binding, rebinding, prebinding, or sold prebound as such a unit, and not requiring special handling. (See definitions.)

3.2 *Ordinary periodical-volume.*—A series of multileaved, like-constituted, serially numbered graphic units submitted for binding or rebinding into a scheduled multi-unit volume and not requiring special handling. (See definitions.)

3.3 *Special volume.*—Any undersized, oversized or odd-sized volume, or any volume that requires special handling.

4. MATERIALS SPECIFICATIONS

4.1 *Thread.*—

4.1.1 *Machine Oversewing.*—When used for machine oversewing, thread shall be at least equal to that recommended by manufacturers of the machine in quality, construction, and performance characteristics when used in the proper operation of the machine.

4.1.2 *Hand Sewing.*—Thread for hand oversewing shall be of linen, cotton or nylon.

4.1.3 *Side Stitching.*—Thread for books that are side stitched by machine shall be at least equal to cotton thread No. 14-4 cord.

4.2 *Boards.*—

4.2.1 *Quality.*—Board quality shall conform to the requirements of Commercial Standard CS50-34, for solid binders board.

4.2.2 *Thickness.*—The thickness of the board shall be adapted to the size and weight of the volume bound, and shall be between 0.060 and 0.205 of an inch.

4.3 *Cover Materials.*—Cover materials shall be pyroxylin-impregnated fabrics which shall conform to the requirements of Group F buckram of Product Standard PS 9-68 *Fabrics for Book Covers* developed cooperatively with the National Bureau of Standards and U.S. Department of Commerce. Obtainable from U.S. Gov't Printing Office, Washington, D.C. 20402 (10¢).

4.4 *Back Lining for Volumes over ½-inch Thick and All Periodicals.*—

4.4.1 *Fabric.*—The fabric shall be cotton, thoroughly cleaned, free from waste, and may be napped on one side.

4.4.2 *Weight.*—The weight of the fabric shall not be less than 4 ounces per square yard.

4.4.3. *Weave.*—The weave shall be plain.

4.4.4 *Yarn.*—The yarn shall be single ply.

4.4.5 *Thread Count.*—The thread count per inch shall be not less than 45 in the warp and 38 in the filling.

4.4.6 *Breaking Strength.*—The breaking strength (by the strip method) shall be not less than 42 pounds per inch for the warp and 53.5 pounds per inch for the filling.

4.5 *Back Lining for Volumes ½-inch Thick or Under.*—

4.5.1 *Fabric.*—The fabric shall be cotton, thoroughly cleaned, free from waste, and may be napped on one side.

4.5.2 *Weight.*—The weight of the fabric shall be not less than 2.5 ounces per square yard.

4.5.3 *Weave.*—The weave shall be plain.

4.5.4 *Yarn.*—The yarn shall be single ply.

4.5.5 *Thread Count.*—The thread count per inch shall be not less than 33 in the warp and 25 in the filling.

4.5.6 *Breaking Strength.*—The breaking strength by the "grab method" shall be not less than 44 per inch for the warp and 40 per inch for the filling.

4.5.7 *Alternative.*—The back lining for books over ½-inch thick may be used in volumes ½-inch thick or under.

4.6 *Inlays.*—All covers shall have an inlay of flexible paper, with the grain running lengthwise, securely attached to the inside of the backbone of the cover. The paper shall be of a thickness appropriate to the thickness of the cover boards, but not less than 0.012 inch, and no thicker than 0.025 inch, except in the case of periodicals where it may be not more than 0.030 inch.

4.7 *Reinforcing Fabric.*—Reinforcing fabric for end papers shall be standard 80 x 80 thread count print cloth construction, prorated to 39 inches, 4.00 yards per pound.

4.8 *Special Reinforcement.*—Special reinforcement shall be used for end papers for heavy, bulky, or large volumes in accordance with their special needs.

4.9 *End Papers.*—End papers shall consist of three functional parts: a pasted-down or outward endleaf which becomes the cover lining, at least two free flyleaves and reinforcing fabric. For books and ordinary periodicals, they shall be a basis 24 x 36—500, 60 lb. and meet the following requirements:

*Folding Endurance M.I.T. Machine**		*Tensile Test Testing Machines, Inc.*		*Tearing Test Elmendorf*	
With Grain (MD)	Across Grain (CD)	With Grain (MD)	Across Grain (CD)	With Grain (MD)	Across Grain (CD)
Folds	Folds	lb. per 1-in.-strip	lb. per 1-in.-strip	lb. per 1-in.-strip	lb. per 1-in.-strip
200	275	40	25	140	144

* Massachusetts Institute of Technology
(MD)—Machine Direction
(CD)—Cross Direction

4.10 *Gold.*—Gold shall be genuine X.X. 23-carat. (Foils and inks are not specified, but shall be such as will insure legible lettering during the life of the binding.)

4.11 *Glue.*—Glue for back shall be a high-grade, flexible adhesive, either animal or polyvinyl resin.

4.12 *Paste.*—Paste for casing-in shall be glycol, polyvinyl resin, or an equal nonwarp paste.

5. MANUFACTURING SPECIFICATIONS

5.1 *Collating and Mending.—*

5.1.1 *All Volumes.—*All volumes shall be carefully examined before being taken apart to detect any peculiarities of paper or construction in order to determine the most suitable method of binding or the necessity of special handling, or a determination that library binding is inadvisable.

All volumes shall be collated page by page before binding, in order to determine completeness and nature of material, to diagnose material, sewing and other treatment, and to arrange material in proper sequence preparatory to sewing.

In Prebinding, where new copies of a title are purchased in quantities, such collating shall be made as is necessary to insure the completeness of the books.

5.1.2 *Periodicals.—*With respect to periodicals, the following additional processing is required:

5.1.2.1 *Collating.—*All issues shall be carefully checked issue by issue and page by page and collated for proper sequence, pagination in accordance with publisher's arrangement, and to be sure that title page, index, inserts and supplements are included. Incompleteness or defects shall be reported.

Volumes not collated in accordance with these specifications shall not be represented as LBI Standard.

5.1.2.2 *Instructions.—*Inclusion or omission of covers, advertising, and similar material shall be handled in accordance with library or customer instructions.

5.1.2.3 *Special Checking and Collation.—*Foreign language and technical periodicals shall be given such special checking and collation as may be necessitated by the nature of the contents.

5.2 *Tears.—*All tears shall be mended with Perma-film, or its equivalent. Margins shall be pieced out with bond paper, high-grade book paper of suitable weight, or their equivalent. No volume shall be prebound which is torn or otherwise imperfect.

5.3 *Preparation for Sewing.—*

5.3.1 *Double Leaves, Maps, Inserts, and Folded Sheets.—*All double leaves, maps, inserts, and folded sheets shall be set out with strips of bond paper, or its equivalent.

5.3.2 *Reinforcement for Sewing.—*Volumes to be rebound and periodicals which are unsuited for oversewing or side stitching shall be prepared and reinforced if necessary, for sewing through their folded sections.

5.4   *Removing Backs.*—

5.4.1   *Volumes.*—For volumes that are to be oversewed, where margins allow, folds on the back shall be removed so as to leave all back margin possible. Where margins are inadequate, the original sections are to be used, unless they exceed the thickness provided for herein, in which event the sections shall be split to conform to the thickness specified in Section 5.5.

5.4.2   *Periodicals.*—Periodicals that come wire stitched in bulky "saddle" style, and which have excessively narrow margins, shall be prepared for oversewing by being slit with a knife by hand or machine (instead of being sanded or cut off).

5.5   *Dividing into Sections.*—Volumes that are to be oversewed shall be divided into uniform sections, each section not to exceed 0.055 inch in thickness, except those of flexible, pulpy paper which may be in thicker sections not to exceed 0.065 inch each.

5.6   *Scoring.*—All sections of volumes in which paper is moderately stiff shall be scored before sewing, unless the paper is not suitable for scoring. (Stiff papers unless hinged shall not be oversewed; usually these may be sewed through their folded sections after necessary reinforcement of folds.)

5.7   *End Papers.*—All end papers shall be fabricated into a unit, with the grain of the paper running lengthwise and consisting of three functional parts: a pasted-down or outward end-leaf, at least two free flyleaves, and reinforcing fabric. The following two types of end papers and their construction are indicated:

(a) Type X: Three-leaf, single reinforcement, invisible joint, with the inward flyleaf not pasted to the middle leaf.
(b) Type Y: Three-leaf, single reinforcement, visible joint, with inward flyleaf not pasted to the middle leaf.

Manufacturers of end papers shall warrant in writing to their customers that the material used in end papers, including the paper and the reinforcing fabric meets all the specifications contained in this standard for end papers and reinforcing fabric.

5.7.1   *Construction of End Papers.*—The construction of end papers shall be such that the sewing will go through the reinforcing fabric the same as through the sections of the book, and the end paper with the reinforcing fabric shall be folded and tipped so as to hinge from the binding edge.

5.8   *Sewing.*—

5.8.1 *Volumes Having Proper Inner Margins and Suitable Paper.*—Volumes having proper inner margins and suitable paper shall be sewed with thread by the oversewing method, either by machine or by hand. If sewed by machine, all sections shall be pasted. As many needles shall be used as possible, providing that this does not bring the sewing closer to the head and tail of the book than ¼-inch after trimming.

5.8.2 *Exceptional Volumes.*—Exceptional volumes requiring flat opening such as music, certain art books, some periodicals with narrow margins or stiff paper, and some reference books, shall be sewed through their folded sections. When such sewing is used, weak folds of sections shall be reinforced with strips of bond paper, loose leaves hinged in, and the sewing shall be done on two or more tapes or cords, with linen thread, usually one-on. For example, volumes 8 inches up to 14 inches require three cords; volumes 14 inches or over require four cords.

5.8.3 *Volumes ½-Inch or Less in Thickness.*—Volumes ½-inch or less in thickness may be sewed side stitched by machine, or by hand, provided that when sewed by machine a volume shall have as many stitches as the machine can employ, and, in any event, whether by hand or by machine, stitches shall be approximately ½-inch apart, with distance between stitches defined as the open space between the thread stitches measured on the inside of the signature; the length of the stitch is the length of thread visible on the inside of a sewed signature. Stitches must come to no more than ½-inch from the top and bottom of the volume, and the sewing shall not extend more than 5/32-inch in from the back edge of the volume.

5.8.4 *Special Arrangements.*—Special arrangements, wherever necessary, shall be made with the library as to the sewing or other handling of all volumes which are originally bound by spiral, plastic or similar methods.

5.9 *Trimming.*—When volumes are trimmed, the trimming shall be as slight as possible. Periodicals shall be trimmed to sample, or recorded sizes, where possible; otherwise, as slightly as possible. The knife used for trimming shall be free of nicks that create burrs, so that edges will be smooth.

5.10 *Gluing, Rounding, Backing.*—Backs of volumes shall be glued with flexible adhesives, well rounded and backed.

5.11 *Lining.*—Backs of volumes shall be lined as follows: *either* with back lining material extending to within ½-inch of head and tail of volumes and onto each end paper at least

1¼-inches, *OR,* if the end leaf reinforcing fabric extends onto the board 1¼-inches, the back lining need not extend onto the cover more than ¾-inch. All volumes over 2½-inches in thickness or 5 lbs. in weight shall be reinforced with tough back lining paper upon the fabric lining covering the entire backbone.

5.12   *Covers.—*

5.12.1   *Material.*—Covers, including illustrated covers, shall be made of heavyweight, pyroxylin-impregnated buckram of a quality at least equal to the standards set forth in section 4.3 of this Standard. Manufacturers of illustrated covers shall warrant in writing to the library binder that the buckram is of a quality at least equal to the standards set forth in section 4.3, that the paint and ink used therein is abrasion resistant and will not crack or peel.

5.12.2   *Board.*—Covers shall be made over hard-rolled binders board, with uniform squares and proper joints, in a neat and workmanlike manner. The thickness of the board shall be suited to the size and weight of the book. (See Section 4.2.)

5.12.3   *Turn-in.*—The cover material shall be uniformly turned in enough to insure proper adhesion (normally ⅝-inch to ¾-inch on all sides is necessary).

5.13   *Inlays.*—All covers shall have an inlay of flexible paper, with the grain running lengthwise of the inlay and securely attached to the inside of the backbone of the cover. The paper shall be cut approximately the same width as the back of the volume after it has been rounded and backed and at least as long as the cover boards. The paper shall be of a thickness appropriate to the thickness of the cover boards, but not less than 0.012-inch, and no thicker than 0.025-inch, except on periodicals where the thickness may be not more than 0.030-inch.

5.14   *Casing-in.*—Volumes shall be cased with glycol paste or polyvinyl resin and either pressed between metal-edged boards until thoroughly dry, or processed through a Building-In Machine with sufficient pressure on the book to insure good adhesion of the end papers and sufficient pressure, dwell (as recommended by the manufacturer of the machine) and heat on the Nippers to form the cover and insure good adhesion in the joints.

5.15   *Lettering.—*

5.15.1   *Gold.*—Lettering shall be done in clear type of a size appropriate to the book and in style and position as instructed, using X.X.23-carat sized gold deeply impressed to insure long adhesion to the cover.

5.15.2 *Colored Foils or Inks.*—Colored foils or inks may be used; but no gold-colored substitute of any kind may be used, without the specific approval of the customer.

5.15.3 *Periodicals.*—With respect to periodicals, binders shall keep necessary records by which uniformity of sets may be maintained.

5.16 *Protective Coating of Volumes.*—Unless specified by the customer, no books shall be sprayed or treated with a protective material over their lettered backs.

5.17 *Inspection.*—For Quality Control, all volumes shall be carefully opened out and critically inspected under supervision, to insure adherence to this Standard and to maintain quality control.

6. SPECIAL VOLUMES

The binder and customer shall agree as to the nature of the special work to be done, or the binder shall exercise his best technical judgment as to the requirements of a particular special volume. No effort is made in this standard to cover all kinds of special work, but the approved methods of processing most kinds of library work are indicated.

7. DEFINITIONS

All along.—A process in hand sewing of books, with the thread passing from kettle stitch to kettle stitch of successive sections, one complete course of thread going to each section. Also called *one sheet on,* and *one on.*

Back or backing.—The process of shaping a ridge or shoulder on each side of the back of a sewed volume, prior to covering, by way of compensation for the thickness of the boards, and to provide a hinge-line from which the cover swings without strain.

Back edge.—The left-hand edge of a recto, corresponding to the right-hand edge of a verso. This is the binding edge in the case of the ordinary bound volume.

Back lining.—Generally, the material (paper or fabric) used to line the back of a book prior to encasing it in a loose back (or hollow back) cover.

Backbone.—That portion of a bound volume which stands exposed when ranged with others on the shelf, cover to cover, in the usual way. Also called *spine* and *shelf back.*

Binders board.—A high-quality, single-ply, solid-pulp board for bookbinding, made to full thickness in one operation from mixed papers, and kiln-dried or plate-dried. Sometimes called *millboard.*

Buckram.—A filled book cloth with a heavy-weave cotton base. Originally applied only to a starch-filled fabric of this type; now, applied to an impregnated fabric with a heavy base.

Casing-in.—The process of putting a volume that has received all of the binding or rebinding operations into its cover or case.

Collate.—In library binding, to examine a book or periodical volume, page by page, before binding, in order to determine completeness and nature of material, to diagnose material, sewing, and other treatment, and to arrange material in proper sequence, preparatory to sewing.

End papers.—That part of the front and back of each library bound volume which attaches the volume to its cover.

Filler.—The material used to fill the interstices, i.e., starch, china clay, pyroxylin or other nonfibrous materials.

Filling.—The threads that run crosswise of the fabric from selvage to selvage.

Flyleaf.—(1) A blank leaf at the beginning or the end of a volume, between the lining paper and the first or last section. (2) Loosely, also the blank free half of a lining paper or a blank leaf which is part of the first or last section.

Foil.—Leaf used in stamping lettering in various colors.

Fold.—A bond in any flexible material, such as paper, made by turning a sheet over upon itself.

Full binding.—The binding of a book completely (both back and sides) with any one material. Strictly speaking, this term, and also the term *full bound,* should apply only to leather bindings. Also called *whole binding.* See also *half binding,* and *three-quarter binding.*

Half binding.—A style of binding having a leather back and leather corners, and cloth or paper sides. The leather of the back should extend onto the boards one-quarter of the width of the board, and the corners should be in harmonious proportion. The term *half binding* is applied also to any similar combination of two different materials.

Head.—(1) The top of a volume or page. (2) By extension, the top portion of the backbone of a bound volume.

Hinge.—Any paper or muslin stub or guard that permits the free turning of an insert, leaf, section, or map.

Impregnated.—A term commonly used for *filled* in the case of pyroxylin-filled fabric.

Inlay.—In library binding, the paper used for stiffening the backbone of the cover. Commonly, but erroneously, called *back lining* or *backstrip.*

Joint.—That part of the cover which forms the hinge and occurs between the board and the shoulder of the volume.

Kettle stitch.—A stitch used in book sewing, by means of which each section is firmly united to the preceding one at head and tail. Also called *chain stitch.*

Library binding.—(1) Volumes bound according to this standard whether rebinding of new or used volumes, prebinding of new volumes (also called prebounds, pre-library bound), and binding of periodicals, as distinguished from publishers' edition binding, library edition, or other binding not in accordance with this standard; (2) The process used in producing binding according to this standard.

Monograph.—For library binding purposes: A separate treatise or thesis on a single subject; when two or more are bound together, a periodical.

Nipper.—(1) A machine that compresses the swelling out of a book. It also squeezes the air out so that the folds are sharp. (2) A machine that squeezes the joint in casing-in.

One on.—See *All along.*

Ordinary book-volume.—Any ordinary-sized graphic material consisting of an appreciable number of leaves or folded sheets produced originally as a unit and submitted for binding, rebinding or prebinding as such a unit and not requiring special handling. (An ordinary book-volume ranges in height from about 6 to 12 inches, with width in proportion and thickness not exceeding 2 inches.)

Ordinary periodical-volume.—A series of multileaved, like-constituted, serially numbered graphic units submitted for binding or rebinding into a scheduled multi-unit volume and not requiring special handling. (An ordinary periodical-volume ranges in height from about 8 to 16 inches, with width in proportion and thickness not exceeding 2½-inches.)

Oversewing.—The process of sewing, by hand or machine, through the edge of each section in consecutive order, using preformed holes through which the needle passes.

Paste-down.—That half of the lining paper which is pasted to the inner face of the cover. Also called *board paper.*

Perma-film.—Self-adhering and transparent material used for covering and protection of pages.

Prebinding (also called prebounds, prebinds).—(1) New volumes bound according to this standard as distinguished from publishers' edition binding, library edition, or other binding not in accordance wtih this standard. (2) The process used in producing binding of new volumes according to this standard.

Recto.—The right-hand page of an open book, usually bearing the odd page number. Also, the front of a separate printed sheet; e.g., of a broadside. Formerly called *folio recto.*

Reinforcing fabric.—A fabric used for strengthening the end papers at their hinge.

Saddle stitching.—The process of stitching together leaves (double leaves inserted one within the other) with the thread or wire passing through the bulk of the volume at the fold line. So called from the saddle of a stitching machine. (See *Side stitching.*)

Score or scoring.—In library binding, making a crease near the edge of a section or leaf, in the case of stiff paper, to facilitate easy opening of the volume.

Section.—In library binding, a group of leaves of a volume, suitable for sewing, not exceeding 0.055 inch thick, except those of flexible pulpy paper which may not exceed 0.065 inch each.

Side stitching.—The process of stitching together single leaves or sections near the binding edge, with thread or wire, from front to back through the entire thickness of the leaves or sections. Distinguished from *saddle stitching.* Also called *flat sewing* and *flat stitching.*

Sizing.—The process of applying a suitable bond between binding material and lettering.

Sprinkled edges.—Book edges on which color has been irregularly sprinkled or sprayed.

Squares.—The portions of the edges of a book cover that project beyond the paper body of the book.

Stained edges.—Book edges that have been stained with color.

Stippled edge.—The edge of a volume which has been spotted irregularly with ink or dye.

Tail.—(1) The bottom portion of the backbone of a bound volume. (2) The bottom portion of a page.

Tapes.—Pieces of tape or strips of cloth to which sections are sewed, and whose free ends are pasted to the boards, or inserted between the split boards of the book covers to lend strength to the binding.

Three-quarter binding.—Binding similar to half binding, except that the leather extends further on the sides, theoretically to three-quarters of half the width of the sides. Corners are proportionately large.

Tip in or tipping in.—The process of pasting a leaf (or leaves) onto a printed sheet or into a bound book, without guards.

Verso.—The left-hand page in an open book, usually bearing the even page number. Also, the back of a separate printed sheet. Formerly called *folio verso.*

Warp.—The threads that run the long way in fabrics, that is, parallel to the selvage.

APPENDIX 1

CONSERVATION OF LIBRARY MATERIALS, George Daniel Martin, Cunha (Scarecrow Press, Metuchen, N. J., 1967)

Chapter I

Historical Background

(Books)—compact compositions of fairly well defined contents and considerable length, possessing cultural, historical or literary significance. *Testaments of Time,* New York, Alfred A. Knopf, 1965.

A book is a book, but its form is ever changing. Neither its physical shape nor its material are in any way fixed. The term properly includes prehistoric rock carvings and scratchings on bone and antlers, ostraka, painted hides, carved amulets, notched sticks, runic calendars, clog almanacs, bronze plaques and many other artifacts on which men since earliest times have left a story in pictures, phonetic symbols, carved letters or writing. It is only a matter of convention that sound recordings and tapes, film strips, and microfilms and cards are not called *books.* From a practical point of view, however, it is useful to consider as books the codex and those forms which closely antedated it in the West or have persisted as record keeping devices in the East almost to the present. These include clay tablets, papyri, linen, silk, leather or parchment scrolls, waxed writing tablets, bundles of palm leaf strips, slips of wood and ivory or sheets of bark.

The Saxons wrote runes on pieces of beech board. The derivation of the English word *book* is from the Anglo-Saxon *boc, bece, beech.* The Latin word for book, *liber,* is derived from the Latin for bark, once used almost universally as a writing material. The Greek word for book, *dipthera,* means skins, which were often used in ancient times.

Regardless of the form or materials of their books, collectors and librarians have always had the problem of preservation. Deterioration of books is not unique to the twentieth century. The early Mesopotamians were bothered by bookworms (earth worms) which bored tunnels through soft clay writing tablets before they were hardened in the sun and even nibbled the surface of the baked tablets, defacing the markings. Clay tablets were easily chipped and broken by rough handling, and to preserve these *brick books,* they were sometimes stored in covered jars. The jars were labeled with clay markers affixed with straw and were shelved in an orderly manner. Records of major importance received even greater protection; for example, some Assyrian terra cotta tablets now in the British Museum were encased in clay wrappers that had to be broken before the records could be reached. It can be argued that these clay covers functioned as envelopes, but since each wrapper bears an inscription similar to that on the tablet within, it seems more logical to call them book covers. Sargon I, founder of the Semitic Empire in Chaldea, established a library of clay tablets which existed until the fall of Nineveh, when it was destroyed by burning.

In ancient China, before the invention of paper, wood was the favorite writing surface except for silk. Narrow slips of wood, originally bamboo, were used for all kinds of records. For lengthier communications these bamboo and wooden slips were joined together at their long edges. They could be conveniently folded into rectangular bundles for storage. Elsewhere in the East custodians soon learned to protect fragile palm leaf books by fastening strips of wood to each side of the bundles of palm. When ornamentation was desired, carved ivory was often substituted for the plainer wood.

Clay was not available in the Nile Valley so the early Egyptians used their abundant papyrus to manufacture a paper-like material. Although superior to clay for writing, papyrus was less durable. For convenience, the papyrus sheets were glued into long strips which were then rolled on wooden cylinders and wrapped in skins or cloth. It is not known when the Greeks adopted papyrus for their books and records. They could have received the knowledge through the Phoenician/Syrian port of Gebel (Byblos) at about the same time they odopted the Phoenician alphabet. The Greek word for book, *dipthera,* suggests that they first used skins for writing, but according to Herodotus, by 500 B.C. papyrus was the preferred material on the Grecian peninsula.

The library of Rameses II (1200 B.C.) undoubtedly contained books made of all of the library materials available to the Pharaohs at that time: clay from other lands, papyrus, palm leaves, wooden pallets, bark, linen, skins and stone. Parchment did not come into use until much later, about 200 B.C. With the exception of stone, all were vulnerable: clay to worms; papyrus to insects, moisture and desiccation; bark, wood and palm leaves to termites; skins and linen to rot and to the cockroaches, silverfish, beetles and mud wasps that infested that hot, dry land. For protection against vermin, dirt and dampness, the Egyptians, Greeks and Romans stored their tightly wrapped scrolls in cylindrical boxes of wood and ivory.

Scrolls continued in common use for centuries and the techniques for making these volumes are well documented. When an author finished his manuscript, it was copied as many times as required by the *librarii,* or transcribers, and the copies sent to the *librarioli* who ornamented the texts and supplied the titles and colophons. The scrolls then went to the *bibliopegi* who bound them by cutting even margins and square ends then polishing the blank sides with pumice. Next they attached wooden cylinders at each end for rolling and added a title, either by affixing a tag to one of the wooden rolls or by pasting a label to the outside of one end of the scroll. Decoration was plain or elaborate, according to the importance of the text or pride of ownership. Catullus describes a book bound for a poet named Suffenus as follows:

> His paper is royal, not common or bad
> His wrappers, his bosses are totally new;
> His sheets, smoothed by pumice, are all ruled with lead,
> And bound with a ribbon of rose colored hue.

Later, in the Alexandrian Library and in others in Greece and Rome, after parchment and vellum had become common writing materials, the conservation problem eased somewhat because of the greater durability of lime-treated skins.

As recorded knowledge increased, the problems of storage increased in proportion. Even under ideal conditions, scrolls were not easy to handle or shelve and in excessively moist or dry areas there were serious conservation problems. A dry tightly rolled parchment crumbles when unwound. Excessively moist parchment cockles badly, defacing any writing on it. Hence it was only natural that those concerned with the making and keeping of records and books should investigate alternatives to the scroll and the *codex* form began to emerge.

It is generally agreed that shortly before the emergence of Christianity, when desk type furniture was first used in Greece and Rome, writers began to use oblong sheets for convenience. These, after being inscribed, were gathered into bundles and fastened along one edge by sewing. The few papyri extant today in codex format are stabbed at one edge and laced through the stabbed holes. This is a clumsy method of binding and is very hard on the pages. Perhaps that is why early record keepers soon resorted to fastening their pages with glue. Cicero, in his *Epistles to Atticus* (56 B.C.), has an orator ask a friend for two of his librarians who might "conglutinate" his books. This could mean to glue the papyrus sheets into rolls, but it is interpreted by others as evidence of the early existence of books in codex form. There are also indications that the early Christians favored papyrus sheets over parchment rolls for reasons of economy.

Another influence in this evolutionary process was the popularity among scribes of the Roman *pugillaria*. These wax-coated wood or ivory writing tablets were convenient in size and had a firm writing surface. Even when two or more were hinged together (diptychs and triptychs) to record lengthy data, they were easy to handle and, more important, the written surfaces, pressed flat when the book was closed, protected each other.

Another factor was the increased use of parchment because of the ever increasing scarcity of papyrus. Papyrus sheets could be fastened end to end in rolls or in bundles by a combination of edge stabbing, sewing and gluing. Parchment, on the other hand, did not roll easily and when edge bound, the sheets in the books so formed did not fold back easily. A more practical method of binding was soon devised. The scribes folded rectangles of parchment down the center, inserted several of these folded sheets within each other to make a gathering of pages and then sewed through the common center fold exactly as single signature note books are made today. The next logical step was to fasten several of these sewn gatherings together by chain stitching at their spines (folds) to make books of as many pages as were necessary.

As this new book form increased in popularity, it became apparent
that chain stitching, while suitable for thin volumes, was not strong
enough for books of a dozen or more gatherings. The spines would
cave in as do thick, cleaply made volumes today. Sometime around
500 A.D., probably in a monastery workshop, an inventive binder developed a technique for fastening the gatherings of vellum pages to
several cords as well as to each other and bonding the sewn gatherings
by applying glue to their common back. This resulted in a book that
would hold its shape, open and close easily, lie flat when open and,
above all, provide maximum protection for the written pages.

The folding of pages, gathering them together, sewing the gatherings
to cords or vellum slips and then gluing is basically the same as modern
binding of Western books. All subsequent operations are to provide
protection for the binding or to decorate the protective covers. The
simplest and most obviously needed protection was to glue a skin over
the spine to protect the exposed cords and sewing. There was also a
need to protect the sides from wear and tear, dirt and dampness. Extending the leather spine covering over the sides helped, but boards
were better. At first the boards were simply glued to the leather at the
joint, but it was soon realized that the cords to which the pages were
sewn, if long enough, could be laced into the protective boards. This
securely fastened them to the book, formed hinges for the covers and
made a rigid base for subsequent covering. The protective leather
could then be cut to the taste of the owner, either to cover only the
spine and the joint or to extend entirely over the boards. The net result was a durable volume that not only protected the manuscript, but
also was pleasant to handle, handsome in appearance and well suited
for subsequent decoration. This new binding technique spread rapidly
through the Western Mediterranean countries and Europe, and is still,
with little change, used by fine binders in Europe and America. Ex-
perimentation with new materials, minor innovations in sewing technique, clasps and ties, headbanding, etc., are all merely variations of
the basic binding technique originated by ingenious craftsmen 1500
years ago.

The Greeks and Romans, and later the Byzantines, were much interested in the decoration of books as well as their form. Sumptuous
bookshops existed in the major cities and bibliophiles sought out skillful book makers. In one of his letters Cicero requested a friend to send
him two slaves who were very clever binders. The evidence from Pom-
peii, Herculaneum and elsewhere is that many book collectors had
large libraries of beautifully bound and exquisitely decorated volumes.
In Greek and Roman times these were mostly scrolls, many in protective cases. Later the Byzantines added elaborately decorated and
jeweled codex form books to their collections.

In the Near East, the codex developed along slightly different lines.
There craftsmen emphasized lightness and suppleness as distinguished
from the more massive oaken boards and thick leather covers of the
West. The Islamic practice, still in use today, is to protect sewn gatherings of pages with thin wallet-type covers of leather, sometimes
stiffened with cardboard, pasted to the spines. Often a fabric liner is
inserted between the spine and leather to reinforce the hinge. No cords
are used in the sewing to stiffen the spine, support the gatherings or
to fasten the boards. The flap extending from one cover around the
fore-edge and tucking into the other cover is a distinctive feature. This

Islamic style culminated in the great school of binding in Persia in the fifteenth century, which in turn greatly influenced European craftsmen.

Far Eastern civilizations developed independently their own variation of the codex: the *orihon,* which is still in use in China and Japan. To avoid the clumsiness of rolled documents, Asiatic calligraphers wrote in short lines along the horizontal axis of strips of writing material, grouping words in about the same way as in modern books. The lengthy strips were folded accordion fashion (making pages that could be flipped over with the fingertip) and these pleated sheets were then stabbed along one edge and laced between protective covers of heavy paper or cardboard. They were easy to handle and shelve, opened easily, could be identified on the spine, and the covers invited decoration. The chief disadvantage was the waste of writing surface on the reverse of each page, which was unusable because of the accordion folding and sewing. Today Chinese and Japanese publishers, in addition to making books which in form and style are very similar to ours, have developed a compromise between the Western style and the orihon. The sheets of paper are printed on both sides, gathered into bundles, stabbed along one edge and tightly laced between protective covers. No adhesive is used on the spine or to fasten the covers to the book. The result resembles the orihon in appearance, but provides the maximum available printing surface.

During the development of the book as we know it, decoration has always kept pace with advances in binding technique. Gold and silversmiths, enamelers, jewelers, ivory carvers, and wood carvers vied with leather workers to ornament the covers of books. Pride of ownership, as well as the desire of craftsmen to demonstrate their skills, resulted in a wide variety of adornments. Many of the very early books still in existence reflect the Byzantine influence by their heavy ornamentation in gold, silver and precious stones. The decorations on monastic bindings were often ornate religious symbols. It is interesting to note, however, that ostentatious decoration was not universally accepted. Saint Jerome, for one, criticized sumptuously decorated books and their owners with this comment, "Your books are covered with precious stones and Christ died naked before the gate of his temple." Nevertheless, when the circumstances of the owners permitted, lavish decoration was often applied. In *Notatia Dignitatum Imperri* (circa 450 A.D.) there are descriptions of volumes of the Emperor's instructions bound in brightly colored leather and ornamented with the sovereign's portrait. The Carolingian influence is reflected in the few remaining examples of the ninth to eleventh-century French books which were often covered with velvet and studded with pearls, gold nails and rubies as well as with tooled leather. Much of the elaborate book decoration during the later Middle Ages resulted from new skills brought back by the Crusaders. It was also at that time that the art of enameling was introduced into Western Europe from Persia through Constantinople.

Although most Celtic book decoration was fairly simple, some volumes belonging to parish churches were kept in elaborate reliquaries. The ornamentation on these shrines (cumdachs) more than compensated for the plain covers on the books. Meanwhile, across the Irish Sea, the English style of bookmaking, which emphasized strength and durability, was coming to the fore. The English, rather than emphasizing plainness, made use of blind stamping (i.e. designs impressed into moist leather with warm tools).

Islamic book decoration was developed from the highly skilled leather crafts of Christian Syria and Egypt. In their period of greatness (600 to 1200 A.D.), the Mohammedan invaders carried their skills and crafts into Europe by way of Spain and Sicily. Islamic ornamentation, until artistic leadership passed to Persia at the beginning of the fifteenth century, was austerely geometric. In Persia elaborate decoration was deemed more suitable to the refined sensuousness of their luxurious and courtly life. Craftsmen in Herat developed the techniques for exquisite filigree work, painted landscapes, all-over gilding and inlaying that spread eastward into India and west through Venice into Europe.

Concurrent with the movement of people and goods in the Middle Ages, came the inevitable migration of the enemies of books. Bookworms and fungi thrived in all the temperate climates bordering the Mediterranean and were not uncommon even in the colder countries to the north. Librarians joined forces to combat the enemy. A thirteenth-century manuscript, "Remedium Contra Vermes Librarum," was widely circulated. In 993 A.D., Sabur ibn-Ardashir's librarians in Bagdad used chemical in an attempt to control termites. At a very early date the Chinese were using "huang-neih," an extract from the seeds of the cork tree, to ward off insects and Chinese law required that this extract be an ingredient in all paper manufactured in the kingdom. In 1221, after papermaking had been established in southern Europe, the Holy Roman Emperor, Frederick II, because of the disastrous effects of moisture and insects on the new material, decreed that all new Acts had to be transcribed on parchment or, if originally on paper, be transferred to parchment within two years. Cedar oil was a widely used insect repellent and, for extra protection, volumes smeared with cedar oil were stored in tightly covered jars. Other early insecticides and protective devices were alum, chests of cypress wood, clay daubing, camphor, pepper, cloves and clove oil, oil of eucalyptus, musk and red myrrh. Most were of little value, but the fact that all these and many others were tried as insect repellents indicates that early librarians were acutely aware of the importance of conservation and made intelligent efforts in that direction. As early as the fourth century A.D., in the first organized Christian monastic community (at Tabenna in Egypt), the concern for books was so great that its founder, Saint Pachomius, made book preservation one of the cardinal rules of his organization.

Wear and tear from normal use was also a problem. To resist abrasion, heavy books, which were normally shelved on their sides and often on top of each other, were fitted with metal bosses on the corners and sometimes in the center of each cover. Fore-edge clasps and ties were used to keep the books tightly closed. These fastenings prevented dust and dirt from sifting between the pages and kept moisture out, thus helping to reduce cockling. The leather flaps on Islamic bindings served the same purpose. To protect their elaborate, costly and delicate covers, French bookbinders made wrappers (chemises) of leather, silk or sandalwood. The Celts across the sea, where living was more austere, gave their books hard use. Owned mostly by churches and often loaned to traveling friars, they were probably exposed to the elements as often as they were under a roof. For protection against dirt, moisture and the rigors of traveling, the churches

had some of their volumes bound as "girdle books." These were unusual in that the leather covers extended about a foot beyond the fore-
edge of the boards and were cut and sewn so that they could be tied in
a knot for convenient fastening to a traveler's belt. The Celts also made
use of "polaires," which were stout cowhide "satchels" with straps long
enough to sling over one's shoulder or hang from a peg at night. These
seem to have originated in the East, coming to Ireland through Gaul.

During the Middle Ages and the Renaissance, in a world where
communication was slow and the time and distance between centers of
learning was great, there was continuous but very gradual improvement
in bookmaking, quality of materials and decorative techniques. Craft
leadership passed from one place to another as cultural, political and
economic conditions changed. By the end of the Middle Ages the
European book had come to be essentially sewn parchment pages, protected by wooden boards that were covered or partially covered with
leather or vellum. Backs were flat and were without decoration or
lettering, but the sides were often stamped and variously decorated.
Ties of leather thongs were used as often as edge clasps. Whereas hides
were used for heavy book coverings, on smaller books the covers were
often parchment or doeskin, devoid of all decoration. Sometimes these
light skins were used as limp covers without boards.

Paper boards came into use early in the sixteenth century along with
the occasional introduction of paper as a covering material on smaller
books. By this time, calf was almost the universal book covering because of its suitability for blind tooling, which had become the vogue.
It was sometimes colored bright red as a change from the monotonous
brown.

The trend in the fifteenth and sixteenth centuries was to smaller
books (the influence of printing) and as librarians acquired more of
them, they were stood on end on library shelves to utilize better the
available space. This established a requirement for identification of the
book elsewhere than on the sides. At first titles and authors were inked
or painted on the fore-edges of the pages of text, but soon it was general practice to letter and decorate the spines. Rounding and backing of
spines, originally devised for strength and to accommodate the boards,
also provided more suitable surfaces for lettering and decoration.
Edge gilding was decorative, but of equal importance was the fact
that it facilitated cleaning of the top edges of standing books and
helped to keep dust and dirt from falling between the pages.

Gold tooling (gilding), with or without blind tooling, appeared on
the scene in the 1500's and had become quite sophisticated by the
1600's. It was also about this time that the usefulness of goatskin and
pigskin for quality book covering began to be appreciated. Goatskin
was popular with craftsmen for inlaying and they began to turn out
beautifully decorated books using a combination of inlaying and gilding. Pigskin was most popular in Germany where it was usually used
over sturdy wooden boards and decorated by blind stamping. White
pigskin on old books is often confused with *alum tawed* skin which
was prepared by an entirely different process. (See Chapter II.)

The changes in decoration over the past three hundred years have
faithfully reflected the changes and refinements in national tastes.
Colored labels first appeared on the spines of books in the 1600's. Silk
headbands, marbled papers, paste papers and woodblock printed papers
were all in use before 1700. One of the most significant innovations in

the seventeenth century was the use of paper sides with leather spines in lieu of all-leather coverings on book boards. In France, at this time, lavishly tooled rich red morocco was very popular, although morocco in other colors had begun to appear.

In the eighteenth century the use of decorated paper for interior and exterior construction became firmly established. Hollow backs made their appearance as did the first "publishers' bindings," which were almost always solid colored paper covers over light weight paper boards and flimsy sewing. The trend toward cost cutting by the use of cheaper materials and shortcuts in workmanship had begun.

In retrospect, up until the beginning of the Industrial Revolution, the most significant events in the development of the book as we commonly regard it were:

a. The evolution of the codex book form in the beginning of the Christian era.

b. The impetus given to bookmaking by the introduction of paper into Europe at the end of the Middle Ages.

c. The printing of books from movable type.

Each had a profound effect on the making of books and simplified some conservation problems while introducing others.

After the adoption of the codex, with its simplification of handling and storage, the general trend in conservation was for the better. Medieval books written on parchment, sewn on vellum cords, laced to wooden boards and covered with tough leather or vellum were reasonably resistant to all of their enemies except man. Parchment and vellum could be cockled and mildewed by exposure to moisture, but with reasonable care this could be controlled. These materials were relatively immune to insects. Oak and other hard woods were not termite-proof, but wooden book boards managed to stand up quite well for hundreds of years. Vegetable tanned and alum tawed skins lasted for centuries.

The advent of paper for bookmaking reduced cost, increased the availability of writing materials and simplified the work of scribes and bookbinders. At the same time, when dampness and unsanitary conditions were the rule rather than the exception, this new material, extremely vulnerable to the ravages of insects and fungi, greatly reduced the average life expectancy of books. The Museum of the Istituto di Patologia del Libro in Rome has on display many early publications with relatively sound leather and vellum covers, but in which the paper contents are either shredded by insects or pulped by mildew.

With the great increase in the number of books subsequent to the invention of printing, there was a corresponding increase in the problems of caring for them. By this time, however, librarians and collectors were well aware of the disastrous effects of dampness and the importance of warding off insect infestations. They recognized the importance of regular cleaning, frequent airing and drying by limited exposure to sunlight; but other than that, the remedies for book deterioration were few and ineffectual. In the eighteenth century learned societies and universities were offering prizes for practical solutions to the insect problem. In 1774 Dr. Johann Hermann was recognized by the Royal Society of Göttingen for his identification of insects injurious to books and for his determination of the parts of books most susceptible to the insects identified and how to repel and kill these insects.

By the late nineteenth century the reasons for book deterioration, with the exception of acid in paper and leather, had been quite thoroughly identified (see Blades—*The Enemies of Books*) but it was not until well into the twentieth century that truly effective protective and curative measures began to appear.

The many changes in technology during the Industrial Revolution made a great impact on the bookbinding craft. Until about 1800, hand binders, without compromising their traditional high standards of quality and workmanship, could easily bind all the books printed. After that time bookbinders, in order to meet the workload and the competition forced upon them by mechanization, were forced to mechanize their own shops, to cut corners in workmanship and to economize on materials. In all fairness, however, it cannot be denied that this has been all to the good except from the point of view of conservation. Fine binding continued, but the emphasis in the larger binderies was on labor-saving machinery in order to meet the ever increasing demand. Librarians and collectors were pleased with the many inexpensive, attractively decorated books on the market and they were all blissfully unaware that the preservation of these same books would be the despair of later custodians. The fact that so many books made and bound in the nineteenth and twentieth centuries soon fell apart can only be attributed to the adoption by the craft of machinery and manufacturing techniques which speeded production, cut costs and improved marketability at the cost of quality.

It began as early as 1774 when Karl William Scheele, a Swedish apothecary, discovered chlorine, which, within a short time, was being used for bleaching paper. This made possible the use in high cost paper of dirty rags that previously could only be used for cheap stock. However, all too frequently the residual chlorine bleaching compounds were not washed out of the finished product. This accounts, in large part, for the situation often encountered by librarians today in which late 18th century book pages made of rag paper and supposedly long lasting and durable have become acid and brittle.

Early in the 1820's, as an economy measure, some paper makers began to add rosin size to their paper pulp during the beating operation (i.e., *engine sizing*) to eliminate the necessity for the hand dipped gelatin sizing of finished sheets. Rosin is a good size in that it reduces the absorbency of paper, as does gelatin, but it adds nothing to paper strength and accounts for much of the brittle brown-stained paper that occurs in nineteenth and twentieth century books.

About 1775 *tree calfing* was introduced as a book cover decoration. Originating in Holland, the fad spread rapidly throughout Europe and across the sea to America. The treatment to achieve the tree-like patterns on leather was discovered quite by accident and utilizes the natural outward warping of book boards before the linings and end papers are pasted down. When book boards so warped are tilted so that the heads are higher than the tails, water sprinkled on them will flow in rivulets towards the center and the rivulets will join in larger streams converging in a central flow near the bottom edge. The design is like the trunk and branches of a tree. If iron sulphate and salts of tartar are then sprinkled on the covers, a chemical reaction will take place, biting into the leather where it is wet and forming a permanent pattern. While tree calfing is pleasing to the eye, the iron and potassium salts introduced into the leather, even in minute amounts, sooner or later break down into acid. There are many examples of tree calf bindings on which the leather does not appear to have been affected but they are almost all of relatively recent date. There are many more examples of earlier vintage in which the leather is disfigured by "pock marks" and is deteriorated to the point where it is useless as a protective covering.

In the 1800's burgeoning new industries using steam for power created a heretofore unknown problem for librarians. Sulphur dioxide, a major ingredient in coal smoke, penetrated the innermost recesses of urban library buildings, where it was absorbed by the leather book covers. Once absorbed, the sulphur dioxide was eventually converted into sulphuric acid, which destroyed the leather fibers and turned the covers into the powdery nuisances so often seen on old books today.

Because of the ever increasing requirement for paper, it was soon necessary to find and use fibers other than linen and cotton for paper pulp. Ground wood, because of its low cost and abundance, was soon in general use. It was a disastrous development. Paper made from "ground wood" pulp has a high lignin content. This complex organic acid soon attacks paper, causing it to darken and become exceedingly brittle. Rare is the library today where there are not hundreds, even thousands, of books in which the paper is not safe to handle because it was made of ground wood. Even "chemical wood" pulp is not entirely satisfactory for book paper because all too frequently the chemicals used in removing the lignin and natural resins in the manufacturing process are themselves not removed. It was not until eight years ago that researchers developed a formula for making durable wood pulp book paper with a long life expectancy.

For hundreds of years prior to the nineteenth century the manufacture of leather had remained almost unchanged. It took months to convert an animal's skin into leather but the finished product was supple, tough, handsome to look at, and above all, lasting and durable. During the 1800's the time to convert skins to leather was reduced from months to days. As a result of this "improvement," the useful life of leather book covers was reduced from centuries to months.

Michael Faraday studied the causes of leather deterioration as early as 1843. Although the problem had been investigated several times since, it was not until about 1930 that it was completly understood. At that time R. Faraday Innes of the British Leather Manufacturers' Research Association began a series of studies on the mechanism and prevention of decay in leather. His findings made possible the manufacture of vegetable tanned leather that is highly resistant to acid decay. The British Museum, using Innes' data, developed procedures for the use of potassium lactate to de-acidify and protect book covers from decay by sulphuric acid. Paradoxically, although acid resistant leather is now available to the book trade, it is rarely used except by specialty hand binders.

An interesting sidelight to some studies of leather deterioration by the Royal Society of Arts in 1901 was the conclusion that an important factor contributing to early deterioration of book covers was that book binders, in order to obtain neatness and to facilitate gilding, were paring the leather excessively. The leather applied to many books was so thin that in a very short time, and with only routine handling, the edges and corners were worn through, the joints split and headcaps torn off.

Sheepskin, never very durable, came into wide use in the 1800's as a cheap covering material for law books and for circulating library books. Manufacturers began to copy good but expensive goatskin by artificially graining and coloring sheepskin. The imitations were difficult to detect short of careful examination in a laboratory. This subterfuge was probably encouraged by the fact that *Russia,* an artificially grained cowhide, had been popular with binders and collectors for almost a hundred years.

As part of the industrial upheaval, the almost complete mechanization of bookbinding was inevitable and should not be deplored. Without the assistance of machinery, binders could never have kept pace with the ever increasing number of books coming from the printers, nor would it have been possible to keep costs within reason. The first bookbinding machine was a rolling press introduced in 1827 to compress folded gatherings of pages before sewing. Since then one machine has followed another until today folding, pressing, sewing, rounding and backing, gluing, cutting, trimming, making covers, gold stamping, fastening the covers to the book and even pasting down the end sheets is all done by machinery. However, there has been a price to pay. Machine sewn books are just not as strong as hand sewn books. Machine sewn books cannot be tightly laced to protective boards. A casing of paper or cloth over cheap cardboard fastened to the spine of a book with flimsy cheesecloth hinges is hardly more than a dust cover. Even the better grades of chemically treated wood pulp paper can be expected to last only a decade or two.

In restrospect, one must conclude that the Industrial Revolution, instead of destroying an ancient craft, created a new industry. Commercial bookbinding should be considered as separate and distinct from *extra binding,* which is the binding of books by hand in accordance with the traditional techniques of the craft, using the finest of materials and with the highest standards of quality and workmanship. There will always be a requirement for fine hand binding and for the skillful repair and restoration of rare and valuable library materials.

APPENDIX 2

THE STREAM OF BOOKBINDING

A Historical Sketch By W. ELMO REAVIS

Reprinted from Pacific Bindery Talk, April, May, June, 1938

Constructing and putting on book covers is today more a matter of eye appeal than of mechanical ingenuity. Nevertheless the mechanical features had first to be evolved. Museum collections of ancient books teach us that book covers were initially employed as a means of protecting the leaves, and for no other reason. Eventually such covers came to receive wording on their exposed areas,—on their fronts, if the books were to lie flat on tables, and on their backs, if the books were to be shelved. With the advent of printing and a consequent great increase in book making, the decorating of book covers became an art. Whether this was in response to a quickened sense of artistic appreciation, or was fostered by competition among the makers and sellers of early books, can not be said with certainty, now that some four hundred years have elapsed since its inception. Classic examples of early book cover embellishment are known to us as the product of Grolier, the Eves, Le Gascon, Derome and a very few others, whose work, in gold leaf impressions on book covers, has never since been surpassed either in appropriateness of artistic conception or in execution.

Almost exclusively, leathers formed the covering material of that early period, and tooling, blind as well as with gold leaf, constituted the medium of expression. The binder who could produce such work rated as something of an artist. He cut his own elemental tools with which he evolved his decorative designs, and was limited in expression only by the material on which he worked, *leather,* and by the form of the object on which he operated, *the completely bound book.* In the trade he was called a finisher; his assistant who constructed the book was called the forwarder.

Possibly the finisher of ancient books would have preferred his book cover to be separable from the book so that he could have laid it flat on a marble slab while he decorated it. This however was impossible, due to the fact that the cover was fabricated step by step as an integral part of the book and could never be removed without dissecting the book. Boards were laced-on by means of the cords or thongs that had been secured to the back of the book in the process of sewing it, and the leather covering, pared thin around its edges and along the joints and made pliably wet and limp with paste, was pressed by hand and appropriate tools onto the back of the book, where it took on the exact irregularities of thongs and book back. Finally the damp pasty leather was pressed onto the boards and turned in around their edges. The resulting cover was necessarily integral with the book.

Occasionally a volume was bound in vellum, instead of usual leather. This material, because of its unyielding nature, could not be shaped to the irregularity of bands across the book back, wherefore the vellum cover remained unattached across its back, giving rise to what we know as the *loose-back* book,—the more usual leather bindings of the period being *tight-back*. The finisher of these early books had always to do his work on the completely bound book, whatever its covering material.

Book making did not vary greatly in its general design nor in its methods of construction for a very long time,—say for three hundred years. Then the advent of a less expensive and more abundant material to replace usual leather coverings,—namely cotton cloth,—brought about the first major innovation in bookbinding. The year 1822 is generally accepted as the approximate date of the introduction of cloth coverings. Up to that time, although the printing press had already made books relatively commonplace, comparatively few books were *bound* until after they had come into the hands of the ultimate owner. Such individual, if he valued a volume, took it to the bookbinder of his choice to be bound and lettered and perhaps decorated in some agreed style, in conformity with the general procedure already summarized. Increasing costs of bookbinding leathers had brought about the use of paper to cover the side boards, and restricted the more expensive material to covering the backs and joints only of many books, giving rise to the term *half-bound*. Such backs admitted of embellishment in gold and blind tooling, while marbling the papers that were used on the board sides relieved their plainness. Books that were not thus privately bound usually remained in paper wrappers, being unsewed folded signatures, as issued by the printer.

With the advent of cloth as a book covering material, considerable changes in bookbinding methods gradually developed, particularly in Britain and our own country. This period marked the beginning of "edition binding," as we know that term. Printers became competitors of bookbinders, instead of the principal contributors to their support. A sharp distinction was soon voiced by bookbinders between *binding* as practiced by themselves, and what they termed *casing* as performed by printers' binderies, or publishers. The well-to-do continued to purchase their book binding to order, but the greater number of readers were glad to buy equally convenient, though less substantial and admittedly quite commonplace-looking books in cloth "cases" of black, brown, green or equally somber color, lettered (usually by means of paper labels) in the simplest possible manner to reveal the title, and sometimes the author.

Michael Sadlier, in his *The Evolution of Publishers' Binding Styles, 1770-1900* (London, 1930), points out that circulating libraries were first established (in England) in the eighteenth century; that copies of

books would be bound up at individual whim and—in a vast majority
of cases—in plain unlettered sheep; and that, as early as 1761, one
man at least had foreseen the supersession of the conventional leather
binding by a style cheaper, less clumsy and (as matters turned out)
directly prophetic of what was to come. Then this writer muses that
"One can only marvel at the conservatism (or power of vested inter-
ests) which kept the mode thus made cheaply available from being
universal for another quarter of a century."

Carrying forward the narrative, Sadlier continues: "Between . . .
1810 and 1820, London, Edinburgh and Dublin saw the establishment
of a definite class of trader, willing to pay an author money for the
mere right to exploit his work and financially able to carry that ex-
ploitation through all the stages of publishing from copyright purchase
to press-advertisement. But of the several phases of publishing as we
know them today, the binding phase lagged behind its fellows in the
movement to centralized control." ". . . commercial bookbinding between 1815 and 1840, in the course of progression from tolerated to
recognized durability, underwent two principal transformations in its
history . . . this quarter of a century was indeed the vital period in
the evolution of binding from ephemerality to permanence." "From
the rough wrappers of the mid-eighteenth century had evolved tailored
but unlettered wrappers and boards of the seventeen-eighties; thence
the laconically labelled boards of the seventeen-nineties and eighteen-
tens; thence again the more informative labels and more carefully constructed boards, with perhaps spines of a different color, or even with
all-over coverings of mottled or marbled paper, and fortified by simple
tapes and backing." ". . . according to a trade circular issued in 1849
by the well-known binder Robert Leighton, his father—Archibald
Leighton of Exmouth Street, Clerkenwell,—put on the market the
first book cloth in the year 1825. This was a stiffened, dyed cotton
material. . . . The title of the book had to be printed on a paper
label and pasted on the spine."

"Wherefore," reasons Sadlier, "let us agree this compromise—that
there is very strong evidence that cloth binding existed in 1821, and
was regularly practiced by one publisher at any rate from that year
forward; that on the other hand, the style was not in any general
sense commercially accessible until 1825."

The invention of book-sewing machines, at first in Germany, where
they initially employed wire* instead of thread, and followed by
thread book-sewing machines of American invention,** contributed
to the revolutionary innovation in bookbinding methods gradually to
be employed in "edition binding." It became evident that lacing-on of
boards could be dispensed with; that cords and their equivalent tapes
could be wholly omitted from machine-sewed books; and—what was
most revolutionary—that covers could be made up *as cases* free from
the books, to be printed in their flat form, and afterward pasted onto
the books, loose-back style, similar in this particular to the construction of ancient vellum-bound volumes. Bookbinders naturally depre-
cated the trend of such practices, but edition binding of this type continued to grow in proportion to its economic appeal.

Prior to the invention of book sewing machines,† there had already
developed two principal branches of bookbinding, with the beginnings
of a third,—namely (1) the original (2) the edition, and (3) most
recent, commercial. The original binding, as already indicated, was the

ancient *hand binding,* and this continues to the present time under the designation of "extra" or "art and craft" binding;‡—poorly patronized and precariously existing in our own country, better supported in Britain, and at its best in Continental Europe. Well-to-do Americans thoughtlessly send their orders for "extra" binding to London or Paris binders, and thus starve our own craft binders. Present day methods of binders doing the *original* (i.e. "extra" or "craft") binding are essentially those that were practiced as far back as four hundred years ago,—with of course the introduction of some mechanical short-cuts,—while methods and styles of embellishment likewise hark back to originals of the same era.

The branch of bookbinding which we have listed as third in the subdivisions developed, is known to us today as *commercial* (or job) *binding.* In its inception it had to do principally with the binding of books of record, including blank books, ruled commercial volumes and the like. Such volumes, usually large and heavy, called for sound construction with "extra" forwarding, but a minimum of embellishment. "Extra" binders, short of orders but thoroughly trained as craftsmen, constituted the most likely early recruits for *commercial binding.*

The character of this branch of the industry has changed with the advent and general adoption of *loose leaf binding,* so that today, although *job binding* continues to exist, and in fact nominally embraces the greatest number of individual shops of any branch of binding in our country, it now finds available only a nominal amount of blank book work. Almost *any* binding that is not embraced in some other well-defined branch of bookbinding rates as "job binding,"—including what blank books there are made, small lots of letter press books that do not reach edition binders, occasional loose leaf jobs that do not go to loose leaf binders, better-bound individual books that do not quite rate as extra bound, magazine binding, and occasional rebinding, in addition to all types of pamphlet binding.

In the stream of bookbinding, *edition binding* was by the beginning of the last century rapidly becoming its most extensive branch. Edition binding, as already indicated, has now departed furthest from the original pattern of bookbinding, has succeeded in the creation of an almost exclusively machine product, has in consequence encouraged much invention of mechanical contrivances for its use, has experimented with all manner of materials for book covers, adopting and popularizing many of them, and withal has raised the standard of moderate-priced books to a level that is (in many instances) approximately artistic.

Sewing machines for the use of edition binders were followed by the guillotine cutter and then the book trimmer, by the rounding and backing machine, by smashers, gluers, and casing-in machines, and by power presses to assure proper sticking together of book and cover.* For cover-making there were invented case-making machines that employed cut sheets of cover cloth; also others that cut the cloth from rolls as the cases were being made,—each case consisting of a sheet of cloth, a pair of boards, and a strip of paper to line the back of the case and thus accommodate it to the loose-back construction that is incident to all cased binding.

Early in the history of edition binding, presses were introduced for stamping in gold leaf by means of plates patterned after printing plates but adapted to being kept hot in the press,—this to relieve the "extra" finisher of tedious and tiring hand work; also to speed up and cheapen production, and to create a product that is interesting and pleasing, and possibly artistic. Embossing, like gold stamping, by means of similar heated presses, widened the field of possible case (cover) embellishment and added something to further enhance the eye-appeal of edition binding. Success in such ventures led to the use of colored foils and non-gold metallic leaves for lettering and decorating cases, sometimes to cheapen them but often merely to attain variety. Then too the printing of cases by feeding them into the ordinary printing press, made possible the use of two or more colors of ink on the case for the enhancement of its appearance. (Printed cases were common as early as 1840, and perhaps earlier.)

Parallel with this development of more attractively stamped or printed *cases* for edition binding, manufacturers of cover cloths have competed in *cloth embossings* (beginning before 1840), in the production of a seemingly endless range of available colors and shades of materials, in a variety of weaves of fabric that assure individuality in the finished cases, and in varying weights of fabric suited to all sizes, types and prices of books that the edition binder is called upon to design and produce.

Then too came the adaptation of cellulose-coated fabrics (long before used extensively in the domain of upholstering) in weights and finishes suited for purposes of bookbinding, best known perhaps as Fabrikoid, but made by several manufacturers under various names. This type of material, with its multitude of finishes and colors, further enhanced the appearance of cases for edition binding. Seemingly they could not be made much more attractive when, some years ago, cloth suitable for lithographing and cloth and inks adapted to offset printing were all developed. Now apparently *anything that can be printed on paper* can as well be put onto cloth, and the possible embellishment of cases in edition binding is limited seemingly only by the limits of printing,—and who can say how far printing may yet go?

This more recent application of lithographing and printing to cloth fabric has popularized a *reversal in the sequent steps* of case-making in certain edition binding, so that whereas the older method involved making the case first and then lettering and decorating it, now the cloth is lettered and decorated first and the case is made subsequently, —an equally simple procedure when once guides are established by which to locate the boards of the intended case. Various adaptations of the general method involved in this reversed sequence of case-making have long been common in *job binding,* this being true particularly for out-size and less usual volumes; but edition binderies seem to have grasped the possibilities of the method only within the past ten years.

It usually fascinates the novice to see a newspaper press as it prints from rolls of paper. It is equally interesting to see rolls of cloth printed in similar manner, so that the cover design of a best seller, repeated perhaps four times across the width of the cloth, is rolling off in two or three colors, ready to go to the case-making machine, there to be formed into finished book covers.*

It is to be recognized that even in *edition binding,* which is the most highly mechanized form of bookbinding and in consequence is the branch that develops and employs *machine-tenders* rather than *bookbinders,* there is still employment for a few *real bookbinders* to produce dummies and samples by proven hand-methods of the craft. No machine is ever set to run an edition until after one or more samples, produced by a real bookbinder, are first made up, bound and approved. In studying steps employed in all branches of bookbinding, it is wrong to assume that the hand bookbinder uses one method to produce a given result, and the machine a different method to produce a like result; the truth is that the machine employs the same fundamental principles and is merely able to turn out the books more rapidly and with greater uniformity.

A branch,—or possibly it should be called a *sub-branch,*—of bookbinding, that is the most recent development in the industry, has already attained maturity and numbers several concerns of national standing which are devoted to its production. Reference is intended to *Superfinish Cover binding* which finds its principal field of employment on school annuals and commercial catalogues. This is really a specialty line of *cover making,* rather than bookbinding in its truer sense, because Superfinish Cover makers distribute the greater part of their product to bookbinders located all over our country. These widely distributed binders send in dummy books, each ready for a cover, and the dummy books furnish the dimensions to which the desired covers are made.

In the present evolution of bookbinding, *cover making* is becoming an increasingly specialized industry in even other than Superfinish Covers. For example several periodicals make a practice of furnishing "cases" to their subscribers who in turn are expected to hand such cases to their job binders for use in binding the periodicals. Likewise cases for binding the *National Geographic* and other popular magazines are distributed on a national scale to various co-operating binders for their use in lieu of locally made covers.

One distinct branch of bookbinding remains to be described, and that is *rebinding,* which takes its name not from its methods or its product but from its principal group of customers. It is called "library binding" and is devoted to the re-binding of the worn books of public and institutional libraries and to the permanent binding of periodicals that come to the libraries in pamphlet binding.

Library binding has appropriated to itself whatever of equipment, methods and materials it has been able to use, from every other branch of bookbinding without let or hindrance. It has little, other than its particular type of machine sewing, that it can call *exclusively its own.* There is however propriety in this state of affairs, because the library binder is called upon to re-bind any and every type of book that has ever been bound,—and he generally succeeds in doing this;— hence he must not be in the slightest restricted from using method, material or equipment that is available to any other branch of bookbinding.

Library binding† was in its formative period a matter of twenty-five years ago. By that time a few binders in this country had set themselves forth as *library binders,* and the work of each could be readily distinguished from the work of every other by certain of its peculiarities. Dissimilarity in sewing was most conspicuous; one binder held to tight back construction while another used the loose back; some of them reinforced joints and some did not; a few sewed on end sheets while others just tipped them on; some used head bands, most

omitted them; some lined backs of books with fabric, others with
paper; a few selected substantial materials, too many used the least expensive materials that customers would accept.

Today there is a well-authenticated nationally-accepted set of specifications for *Class A library binding,* embracing methods and materials,
and binders who observe such specifications are nationally certificated.
This advance and development has come about gradually, and with
accompanying improvement and standardization of methods, materials
and equipment.

The advent of library binding was the occasion of much experimen-
tation in book re-sewing, due to the fact that the second sewing of
books offered the most difficult mechanical problem to would-be library binders; wherefore a considerable number of patents on re-sewing were developed,—notably, the Chivers, the Holloway, the Valters,
the Ward, the Koehler, and several others. Then the introduction of the
Oversewing Machine in the year 1920 displaced all of these patented
hand-sewings, and oversewing remains the standard for library binding to the present time.

Job binding and *extra binding* were the fields of bookbinding from
which library binders earliest came. These branches of bookbinding
are notably dependent upon *hand operations,* and it is safe to say that
no hand operation known to either job binding or extra binding has es-
caped being employed, partially used, or experimented with by library
binders from time to time in efforts to meet some specific rebinding
problem, or to improve the average product, or to reduce the cost of
production. Ingenuity should be the middle name of every library
binder, for he challenges an ever oncoming array of problems that
are continually to be solved in re-binding.

The *library binder* first forwarded his books by hand, as the *extra
binder* continues to do; gradually he borrowed from the *job binder*
the rounding machine, roller backer, gluing machine and spray gun;
while from the *edition binder* he has acquired the book trimmer and
compressed-air press equipment. The library binder first lettered his
books by hand as the extra binder does; in time he developed a way
to employ the job binders' stamping press; then he found himself able
to use (for at least a portion of his re-binding) decorated cases produced by edition binders, on which cases he added lettering by means
of his stamping press; while most recently he has been able to adapt
from the edition binder (for yet another portion of his re-binding),
the *fully lettered and decorated cover cloth* ready to form into the required book case by merely gluing onto it the necessary boards and
liner.

Library binding has metamorphosed through several stages,—*earliest,* the search after sound construction, by which maximum service
from the leaves of the books is attained; *second,* the search after materials of correct strength, neither too weak nor too bulky, by which
a covering adequate for the life of the leaves of the book is provided;
and *most recently,* the search after assurance of an attractive appearance in the finished book, by which the claims of the esthetic are
given recognition.

Most industries may perhaps be likened to a river which acquires its
size and form from the convergence of various smaller streams that eventually run together into a single channel. For instance, consider the sev-

eral branches of manufacturing running together to constitute the great automobile industry as we know it. Bookbinding as a contrasting industry, may be more appropriately likened to the opposite end of the river where that river enters the sea through several channels, as in a delta area. Through a few hundred years this handicraft experienced little change in any particular except annual increase in output; that represented the steady flowing river. Then the channel divided: its largest branch became *edition binding,* undergoing very considerable changes while the original stream continued as *extra binding;* then *job binding* developed as a very irregular channel; *loose leaf binding* followed as a little stream quite unlike the others, and *Superfinish Covers* became another little outlet with distinctive characteristics; while *library binding* completed the delta pattern by tying into all the other branches and feeding from each, rather than forming any independent stream of its own.

Whether bookbinding is to experience yet more subdivisions and outlets, the fostering of further eye appeal without increasing cost, will probably be the principal determinant.

The United States Government Printing Office was equipped with these German machines long before the advent of thread book-sewing machines.

The first Smyth Book Sewing Machine (using thread) was shipped from the factory in 1882.

The Brehmer Book Sewing Machine, employing wire instead of thread, was patented in 1877. The Smyth Book Sewing Machine, employing thread, was introduced in 1882, and this, in its various sizes and models, remains the standard book sewing machine in America.

Library binding is the modern term for *rebinding* when performed according to modern specifications. The *re-covering,* and presumably the *rebinding,* of books, in some form or other, is doubtless as old as *edition binding,* because that relatively insubstantial binding gave rise to the need of rebinding. Michael Sadlier, cited in the first section of this article, quotes from a publisher's circular, dated September 22, 1774, which Sadlier discovered in a contemporary copy of Goldsmith's "Experimental Philosophy," and which reads (in part) "In the course of five years, upward of Fourteen Thousand Volumes have been sold *bound in this manner,* and not One Hundred of them have been returned *to be new covered;* a sufficient Proof of its Utility and Approbation by the Public." Italics are mine, but this statement indicates that re-covering and re-binding were being practiced in a commercial way at least as early as the year 1774.

APPENDIX 3

BOOK SEWING DISTINGUISHED FROM BOOK STITCHING

With Discussion of Principal Methods of Performing Each

BY W. ELMO REAVIS

Reprinted from Pacific Bindery Talk, Nov. 1937—Jan. 1938

Both the *sewing* and the *stitching* of books involve two lines of approach as to the material to be sewed or stitched, and each of these has two principal subdivisions. The lines of approach are (first) penetration through *central folds* of the leaves, and (second) through *edges* of the leaves. The subdivisions are (first) penetration through the *entire book,* and (second) through *sequent sections* to eventually comprise the entire book. Any of these four may be produced both by manual means and by the use of some suitable machine. There are allowable variations of detail in each, introducing minor distinctions; but it will assist in attaining a broad comprehension of the subject if the student attempts to assign each sample that is under consideration, regardless of its minor peculiarities, to one of the four groups mentioned.

All of which means that, with a book in hand, the student of its sewing, or stitching, will attempt to discover whether the threads pass directly through the entire mass, or indirectly through section by section to fasten the whole together. Also he will try to discover whether the thread penetrates a side edge of the leaves, or passes through the fold (or folds) of leaves. Knowing these facts, he can comprehend what is fundamental in all book sewing and stitching. And he may be assisted in retaining such distinctions in his mind through a more discriminating use of the terms *sewing* and *stitching* than has as yet become general. Those who think most clearly on the subject do distinguish these terms.

Webster says: "SEW *(Bookbinding)* To fasten together (the sections) by passing the thread or wire through the central fold of each section in such wise as to secure it to the bands;—disting. from *stitch.*" As to stitch, he says: "STITCH *(Bookbinding)* To fasten together (the sections) by passing the thread or wire through all the sections at once; distinguished from *sew*." Unfortunately these nice distinctions between sew and stitch are not generally observed as they should be by those who bind books or who purchase their binding.

We would like to see the term *book stitching* applied exclusively to that form of book construction wherein the thread passes through the *entire book,* whether such book be limited to a single fold (as in the case of a very thin volume) or consists of many sections, regardless of thickness. We would like to reserve the term *book sewing* to apply to the particular form of construction in which sections (i.e. fractional portions of the book) are individually sewed as distinct steps toward the resultant book, whether such fastening is performed through a fold of each section or through the side edge of each section. Webster's definition almost attains this distinction, but not quite, since it specifies sewing *through the folds* of sections, whereas sections may be as truly *sewed* through their side edges as through their folds. *Doing the book as a whole at one operation is stitching; doing the book step by step is sewing; and both sewing and stitching may be performed through central folds and through side edges.*

STITCHING

Well known illustrations of Book Stitching through the side edges of the leaves include usual wire-stitched magazines, also children's text books when similarly stitched and then often bound in hard-covers. Geographies most frequently constitute typical examples, as also text books stitched with thread on the Singer Sewing Machine or on the McCain Sewing Machine or on similar machines. (Note: Observe that although these machines have adopted the name "Sewing Machine," the work that they do is actually stitching, not sewing.) Thin volumes thus processed can be *stitched* on any "sewing machine" provided such machine is equipped with a needle of sufficient strength to penetrate the mass of paper that constitutes the volume. When the limit of the needle's punching capacity has been reached, punching mechanism or drills are incorporated in the "sewing machine" to prepare holes for the needles.

An unavoidable characteristic of all *side-stitched* volumes is their resistance to free opening. Because the stitched area is held compact and is therefore inflexible, the opening of the book is derived from whatever flexibility there may be in the leaves of paper that constitute the book. A wire-stitched telephone book, for example, being printed on flexible leaves (of newspaper), opens in a usable manner, whereas many a children's picture book, printed on bulky stiff paper and side-stitched with thread (although this makes it slightly less inflexible than if wire-stitched) opens very poorly. Typical examples of side-stitched books at their very best are to be seen in the Orient; the soft crinkly paper in old Japanese books, stitched clear through their backs by hand with silk, falls open in a delightful manner, regardless of (and not because of) their side-stitching. No ordinary American book paper will act similarly.

Well known examples of stitching *through the fold* of the book (as distinguished from the preceding stitching through the *side* edges) are to be seen in the ordinary saddle-wire-stitched magazine, like *Literary Digest,* and in books similarly constructed and then hard-bound. Stitch-

ing through the center fold can readily be done on a Singer Sewing
Machine, and many cheap, thin books, especially those for children's
use, are thus constructed. Such books, to be suitable for stitching, must
be limited to relatively few pages each. The maximum practicable
thickness in any saddle-stitched book is soon reached. Greater thickness
than about one-fourth inch is quite impracticable, not because punches
and drills as used in side-stitching are unavailable, but because of the
fact that page-register in the printing of sheets to be so bound requires
special attention by the printer and that attention increases the cost of
producing the printing. This fact can be ocularly demonstrated by taking a quantity of leaves of paper (say bulking one-eighth inch in thickness) and folding the whole just once; then press the fold firmly together and drive a pin through the side of the whole close to the fold
(say one-fourth inch away); thereafter open out the leaves and observe
the comparative positions of the pin holes in the center sheet and in the
outer sheet. In leaves near the center of the fold the pin holes will be
found very close to the fold; this distance will be discovered to increase to a maximum in the outer sheet; hence printing if placed *uniformly* on any sheet, will be badly out-of-register when such sheet is
folded into a single bulky saddle-stitched book. The alternative would
be for the printer to discover the particular position of each page by
trial and then make up his printing form accordingly, all of which
would greatly increase his cost of production. For this reason, among
others, the saddle stitch is discarded in favor of the sidestitch, as soon
as the quantity of leaves in the book attain much in excess of one-
eighth inch in thickness. A well known example of an excessively
thick saddle-stitched periodical is to be observed in *Commercial and
Financial Chronicle.*

Stitching, whether performed through the *fold* (called saddle-stitch-
ing) or through the *side* (called side-stitching), has as its predisposing
characteristic low cost of production. Its use is therefore indicated for
ordinary pamphlets, whether non-covered or paper covered or hard
bound,—it being understood of course that comparatively few pamphlets are ever hard bound. Convenient book construction presupposes
facility of opening, and *saddle stitching* (unlike side-stitching) has this
quality to its fullest, since no book opens further than freely to and
on its center line of fold, any more than any door opens greater than
a full swing back on its hinges,—unless it be a revolving door, and
nobody has as yet invented a book with revolving pages! But, as already indicated, the maximum thickness that is physically practicable
for a saddle stitched book is very limited,—certainly less than one-
fourth inch. Recourse to the side-stitch is necessary as soon as the
book to be stitched attains more than a nominal thickness, and (as
also already indicated) the opening quality of all side-stitched books,
being wholly dependent upon the flexibility of the paper used in them,
and not at all upon the stitching, if wire be employed, and but little if
thread be employed, such books are commonly unpleasant to handle
and are necessarily subjected to forced opening when used. Consequently they soon become torn in their leaves in the area not far from
their stitching. Children's books, whether picture books or school
texts, present typical examples of volumes whose disintegration is
hastened because of the unyielding characteristic of side stitching used
in their construction.

It must be recognized that side stitching, when performed (as it is) in one operation clear through the book, upon any of the modern machines that are equipped with drills and automatic feed mechanisms, is of necessity less expensive than any book sewing can be produced section by section, however done. Particular care in the selection of paper, to have it of suitable quality and weight and flexible and printed with its grain up and down the leaf, will serve to mitigate the inherent constrictiveness of side stitching, so that reasonable service in the finished book may at times be attained; especially so, if the book is of an ephemeral nature and cheapness of construction is of first importance. No book lover can complacently contemplate a stitched book; to him it is only a make-shift improperly dignified with a hard binding.

Advertisements intended to emphasize the inherent *strength* of certain stitched book construction, in which side stitching through strongly reinforced end-sheets is graphically illustrated, tend to divert attention from the real province and purpose of bookbinding. The fact that any volume may be hung up by its two covers and the weight of a man safely suspended from the mass of its leaves (as graphically shown in certain advertisements) may be quite true without qualifying such books for swings or gymnastic apparatus,—and certainly the illustration does not suggest the one and only justification for binding a lot of leaves into a book: namely, so that those leaves may be preserved as long as possible in their most pleasantly usable form. We have known enthusiasts for some particular form of stitching to throw books with great force against a wall, and to pound with them on the floor, and even to jump on them,—all of which feats might be convincing if one desired to purchase books for any of those purposes. The test of any book stitching is alone to be found in subjecting the book to the service for which intended. If the book opens as well as is necessary, and if it lasts as long as is desired, then its stitching is commendable for the sake of economy; but if the constrictive nature of stitching causes readers to unduly strain the leaves in trying to read them, thus bringing such books to repair or replacement too soon, then the stitching is not actually economical or satisfactory, regardless of how much pounding the volume might be subjected to by way of demonstration, or how many men might swing from its suspended covers.

In re-binding, saddle stitching has but little application, due principally to the fact that before the material comes to re-binding, the folds in which the saddle stitching must be placed,—whether by wire stitches, or by Singer Sewing Machine thread, or by needle and thread manually performed,—are greatly weakened or actually torn. Where saddle stitching is obligatory for desired full flat opening (as in the case of orchestral music which must lie open on a music rack), folds must first be reinforced by means of suitable strips of paper or cloth, after which saddle stitching may follow.

Side-stitching, in re-binding, is seldom if ever justifiable. If the volume is worthy of re-binding at all, a more flexible type of construction should commonly be used. A safe rule is to totally prohibit side-stitching in re-binding; if cheapness is wanted, buy a new copy; if serviceability is desired, suitable sewing must be provided.

SEWING

We now turn our attention to Book Sewing as distinguished from book stitching. In book sewing, use is made of the fact that the book consists of a collection of folded signatures, or equivalent tablets of leaves called book sections. The signature ordinarily develops from folding a printed sheet of paper. A single fold produces four pages (two leaves), spoken of as folio; a second fold in the same sheet produces eight pages (four leaves), spoken of as quarto; a third fold in the same sheet produces sixteen pages (eight leaves), spoken of as octavo. This is the practical limit for satisfactory folding of most modern book papers and is the size of signature most often encountered in works of fiction and comparable books. Thinner papers may be folded once again to produce a signature of thirty-two pages (sixteen leaves), called 16 mo; and there are other possible variations, as 12 mo and 24 mo. In each instance a single sheet by folding becomes a signature, and in a securely sewed book this signature is both individually sewed and at the same time attached through certain features of its sewing to the next adjoining signature, so that the whole forms the sewed book, consisting of articulated sections.

Before going into greater detail, it is desirable to point out that each signature can be sewed through its edge (or inner margin), so as to sew it individually and at the same time attach it as a unit to the next adjoining signature, the aggregation to eventually constitute a complete book. For identification, this particular sewing is known as overcasting, oversewing or whipstitching. These terms connote further distinctions as to detail (later to be described) but are generally descriptive of that book sewing wherein one section at a time is sewed to the next section through inner edges instead of through central folds.

Sewing through the folds, signature by signature, is the most ancient form of book sewing, performed with great care and success long before book sewing machines were even thought of, and as such has no generic name other than "book sewing." I prefer to call it, for purposes of identification, fold sewing, or *book sewing through the folds*. In its ancient form it was performed by employing a so-called sewing bench, whence this sewing receives the name in some localities of "bench sewing." Similar sewing performed by machine is commonly referred to by the name of the machine used, as for example Smyth sewing.

The recognized machine for sewing section to section through their edges to form a sewed book, is known as the Oversewing machine, and it has fixed the distinctive meaning of the term "oversewing," which is really an overcasting done by machine.

Having placed before our minds the two great classes of book sewing (as distinguished from book stitching); namely *fold sewing* and *overcasting,* and recognizing that each of these may be performed either manually or by some machine, it is appropriate to now proceed to a more detailed description of all, under four headings: (1) Fold sewing by hand; (2) fold sewing by machine; (3) overcasting by hand; and (4) overcasting by machine, called oversewing. All of these have the common characteristic of flexibility in the sewed book due to sewing section to section, and are in this respect distinctly unlike book stitching, wherein all of the leaves are fastened in a mass or block. (The saddle stitched book, although it opens equally as well as any sewed book, may be appropriately dismissed from further consideration, due to the fact that its use is of necessity limited to very thin volumes; thicker ones must be side-stitched, as already explained.)

Fold sewing is distinguished from *overcasting* mainly by the fact that in it every leaf opens entirely back to the fold,—in other words the widest possible degree,—and is therefore productive of the most flexible form of book construction. Overcasting, although like fold sewing in the characteristic that it attaches section to section, is distinguished by the fact that opening between successive leaves is only as far back as the line of sewing,—say about three-sixteenths of an inch forward from the binding edge of the leaf, which constitutes the back of the book,—but such opening is augmented by the flexible nature of the back of the book developed from sewing section to section, and by whatever flexibility there is in the paper sewed.

Oversewing finds its justification and necessity of the fragile nature of modern, machine-made book papers. Ancient bookbinders had nothing less substantial than rag papers to sew. When they folded a rag paper it did not break in the fold; when they placed good linen thread in the centers of folded sections, there was so much strength present that the binder could not forecast which would outlast the other, the thread or the paper or the outer leather covering. It was no unusual circumstance for the paper to outlast the other two and come up for a re-sewing in the same folds! Modern wood-pulp papers, and especially the large proportion of such as contain ground wood pulp (which distinguishes newspaper) possess no comparable strength or endurance. Once folded, the fibre is cracked or broken in the fold; sewing threads placed there soon sever the already fractured folds and thus release leaves of used books; then such books come up for re-binding. Stitches passed through the edges of such leaves, if numerous enough and yet not so closely placed as to act as perforations, make more secure volumes than the original fold sewing; hence oversewed books outlast original bindings of modern papers. This fact has given rise to the branch of the bookbinding industry that is known as "library binding," and which depends for its patronage chiefly upon public and institutional libraries that must maintain collections of books for continued service.

The weakened and broken folds of fold-sewed books can of course be reinforced and strengthened for a second sewing through their same folds, and this is common practice as to certain types of books where absolutely flat opening is imperative. But reinforcing the folds is relatively expensive (as compared with oversewing) and the practice introduces certain objectionable conditions in the book, notably an undue swelling in the back, arising from the added material introduced as mending strips. It will be readily understood that if every section were reinforced with a strip of paper of thickness equal to that on which the book is printed, the back of the book would be exactly doubled in thickness, or made impossible of acceptance! In consequence, very thin strips and as few of them as practicable are added, and the book, instead of being made as strong as possible, is reinforced as little as possible prior to re-sewing through the folds.

Referring now to the four headings, already presented, for more detailed discussions:

(1) *Fold sewing, by hand.* This is not only the most ancient, but in several respects the most admirable book sewing ever devised. It came into use as early as the thirteenth century, therefore long ahead of the art of printing; it remains the only book sewing permissible for genuine art and craft bindings. Anciently, it was employed on vellum

books, and later on those made of the only paper then known,—strong
pure rag stock; in modern practice it is indicated exclusively for
choicest hand bindings wherein the better grades of our modern book
papers appear.

Such sewing presupposes the employment of tapes, cords or thongs,
and the sewing on of end-sheets (these usually reinforced), besides
the working (not mere gluing) of head bands onto the finished book.
These details all contribute to the strength of the book and make the
accompanying sewing appear even better than it perhaps is; in other
words, *fold sewing by hand, including the other details of book construction which properly go with it,* belongs to the most desirable form
of book construction that is known. Needless to say, this sewing is
relatively expensive.

Bench sewing (this term is very commonly applied to modern fold
sewing by hand) is distinguished by *kettle stitches,* a designation of
which the derivation is in doubt; as good a guess as any is that it
comes from the German for "little chain." A kettle stitch occurs at
the head and at the tail of each section, where it stands as a lock
stitch tying consecutive sections firmly together; wherefore the back of
the fully sewed book discloses a chain of stitches across head and
tail, at appropriate distances from those extremities. Each section
sewed on the bench should carry a thread (single or double) from
kettle stitch to kettle stitch down its center fold. Such fold, when
opened, presents the illusion of having three or more stitches, instead
of just one. This is due to the fact that the lone thread (or pair of
threads) from kettle stitch to kettle stitch passes out and around each
consecutive tape (or cord or thong) upon which the book is sewed.
Cut one of the seeming stitches and the whole thread will pull out, re-
leasing the entire section which it was designed to hold. Sections may
be sewed *two-on* by alternating the stitches between a pair of sections
sewed at one time, but the practice is to be condemned if a sound
book is desired.

The tapes (or cords or thongs) are thus sewed to and lie across the
back of the book for the primary purpose of forming a means of attachment between the sewed book and the boards of its cover; their
secondary purpose is to supplement kettle stitches in holding the successive sections together. It is well to recognize these purposes, as
there will be occasion to point out the effect of the omission of these
from other sewings to be hereafter described. Thread specified for
bench sewing is uniformly linen, to insure maximum strength with
minimum bulk; the thread in the backs of books swells their backs far
more than persons unacquainted with the art may imagine. Silk thread,
for this reason, is often used for sewing Bibles that are printed on
very thin paper.

Bench sewing is practiced in a limited way in most book binderies,
even where no art or craft binding is attempted. Occasional volumes,
that are not suitable for oversewing or whipstitching, will be sewed
by hand on the bench,—in other words, will be bench sewed through
their folds. But if an edition (even a very small one) is to be done,
it will probably be put onto a Smyth Sewing Machine (the operation
of which is presently to be described). For economy in cost, the occasional volume that requires sewing through its folds will be bench
sewed by hand. In this sewing, tapes or cords across the back of the
book must be employed, and kettle stitches will appear at head and

tail, as already described. In the ancient or craft bookbinding, heavy cords or leather thongs were used, thus giving rise to genuine "raised bands" showing on the backs of the books; but in modern bench sewing the tapes, if used, are of thin cotton construction about five-eighths inch in width, and do not show through the backs of the bound books. Such volumes, if they are to be bound to have the appearance of raised bands, are given false bands made by pasting narrow strips of cardboard across lining or false backs glued within the exposed backs of these books. Cords, if used in place of tapes, are generally let into saw cuts made across the backs of the books, and such cuts are easily to be discovered within the sewed book. Lying within such saw cuts, the cords do not show upon the backs of the finished books. This method of bench sewing is less expensive to employ than is sewing on cotton tapes, due principally to the fact that the saw cuts present gashes through which the sewing needle may be speedily passed. The use of such a method is of course inexcusable in any craft or art binding, though commonly employed in the usual types of commercial binding.

Cords, tapes, bands or thongs, used in connection with fold sewing of books, have (as already mentioned) a dual purpose in the art of book binding; first, in conjunction with the kettle stitches, to hold successive sections of the book together; and, second, to provide a means for attaching the body of the book within and to its cover boards. In all craft and art binding, the thongs or cords are "laced into" the boards; that is, they are passed through holes in the boards, then pasted and hammered down flat. A book so constructed cannot be removed from its cover without first severing the thongs or cords on which it is sewed. Cotton tapes and soft cords, as used in commercial binding, can be laced into their book boards, but are not ordinarily so disposed. Instead they are merely pasted to the flyleaves and those eventually to the cover boards, from which boards they can usually be parted without imposing much strain on them. What is here said with reference to cords, tapes, bands and kettle stitches should be remembered for comparison with details of the type of sewing next to be described.

(2) *Fold sewing, by machine.* This sewing never has kettle stitches and is usually performed without employing cords or tapes, although the latter may readily be included by slowing down the rate of production and consequently increasing the cost. Without tapes, this sewing is to be found in nearly all modern publishers' books; and with tapes, in most books that publishers speak of as reinforced or extra strong.

The earliest successful machines for sewing books employed wire stitches instead of thread. They were of German invention several decades ago, and although long since superseded by machines employing thread, some of them are still in use in Europe. No longer employed in this country, a discussion of such machines here is unnecessary. Old Baedeker Guides were all "sewed" on wire sewing machines, and an examination of one of these books will clearly illustrate wire book sewing.

There are about four makes of book sewing machines for sewing through the folds that find favor in this country. The most common and speediest are known as Smyth book sewing machines; these employ a series of curved needles. Similar machines with straight needles are favored for larger and heavier sections.

It will be recollected that in bench sewing (by hand, of course) the sewing thread passes from kettle stitch to kettle stitch, threading its way first within the central fold of the section, then out around the tape, then back into the central fold, and so on through its full course; also that although threads in the central fold present the appearance of three or more stitches, they are in fact continuous, wherefore cutting one stitch will release all stitches that appear in the given section. Also it will be recollected that in hand sewing, the attachment of one section to the next is limited to two rows of kettle stitches, additional holding of section to section devolving upon the tapes or cords if used.

The first major distinction between book sewing by machine and by hand on the bench is found in the fact that in machine sewing each stitch that lies in the fold of each section is independent from all others in the same fold. This arises from the fact that three or more needles are employed simultaneously to sew the books, each needle being fed from a separate spool of thread. Needle number one, fed from spool number one, sews the first (or upper) stitch in the fold of section number one; it does the same in section number two, and so on until the book is completed. Needle number two simultaneously places a series of stitches paralleling those just mentioned; needle number three parallels with its stitches, and so on according to the number of needles appropriate to the height of the book. No tapes or cords are imperative in machine sewing and none are generally used, although tapes may be included and sewed onto the book simultaneously with the sewing of the sections, and tapes greatly increase the strength of the book, in addition to affording a much more secure attachment to the case (book cover).

The second major distinction between machine sewing (through the folds) and hand sewing (through the folds) is to be observed in the fact that kettle stitches are wholly absent from machine sewing, and that successive sections are fastened together only by the sewing threads (unless tapes be used),—a single thread bridging from stitch to stitch at one end of each stitch, and a looped thread performing the same service at the opposite end of each stitch.

In hand sewing (through folds), the sewing thread should travel along the full length of the first section, back the full length of the second section, along the full length of the third, back the fourth, and so on without variation until all the sections are sewed. Kettle stitches join the sections at their heads and tails, and tapes or cords must be employed. In machine sewing (through folds), each sewing thread crosses the book back, instead of following the section folds, and leaves just one stitch in each section as it so crosses. There are no kettle stitches, and the use of tapes is optional, but there is an attachment of section to section at each stitch, this being necessarily as fragile as the sewing thread used. Hand sewing (through folds) presumes the use of relatively heavy linen thread, unless silk be used to accommodate very thin sections, while machine sewing (through folds) presumes the use of thin cotton thread.

It is to be recognized that as books come to pieces and drop their leaves in the course of service, the sewing threads are not commonly giving way, but the paper is usually parting where folded. Hence a corrective is not to be found in greater thread strength nor even in the inclusion of tapes in the sewing, though that will improve the serviceability of the book,—but is to be found in a sewing that will catch and hold a modern paper elsewhere than in the creases of its section folds which have unavoidably been strained and cracked in the mere process of folding. This brings us to a consideration of the next type of book sewing.

(3) *Overcasting, by hand.* This sewing is frequently called "over-sewing," thus adopting the name originating from the machine on which similar sewing is performed. A real distinction should however be observed between "overcasting" and "oversewing by hand." This latter has a pattern or regularity that is wanting in common over-casting, due to the fact that oversewing is always performed through machine-made holes (stabbings or perforations) placed in the binding edge of each section, whereas in ordinary overcasting the operator must thrust the needle through the paper by hand for each stitch taken. No paper is easy to sew in this way, and the firmer papers are really diffi-cult to penetrate by means of the sewing needle, which fact encour-ages irregularity in stitches both as to their depth and as to their spac-ing apart. The deeper stitches in overcasting invite tears in the leaves when the book is opened, and wide spacing apart of stitches produces an unavoidable weakness in the book. Ordinary overcasting is there-fore to be condemned and avoided, whereas oversewing by hand has a proper place in bookbinding.

As already indicated in an earlier portion of this article, fold sewing, whether performed by hand or by machine, tends to lacerate the sig-nature folds and to render them unfit for re-sewing in a like manner. This fact is the principal reason and occasion for the employment of oversewing in most re-binding, so that the leaves may be secured by an appropriate number of stitches through their sides. The fold-sewed book of fiction size will have four stitches in each section, lying neces-sarily in the crease-weakened fold of the same, whereas each such section when re-sewed by a suitable oversewing method will receive anywhere from a dozen to thirty stitches (depending on the particular pattern of oversewing employed) to hold it in the re-sewed book, thus greatly increasing its strength over its original fold sewing.

The opening quality of the oversewed book will not equal that of the fold sewed book, but will be reasonable and practicable, and even excellent in the case of all flexible papers,—and, needless to say, in-comparably better than if the same book were *stitched*. To improve the opening qualities of oversewed books in which the less flexible papers are used, recourse is had to scoring each section before over-sewing it. Scoring may be performed in any of several ways, but more frequently the library binder employs a scoring machine wherein thoroughness and uniformity are attainable at small cost. The idea in scoring is to fold each section a couple of times to right and to left to flex the paper without going so far as to break the fibre. A relatively stiff paper is thus given a bending quality along the line of its sewing equal to that of a naturally more flexible sheet which requires no scor-ing.

Where oversewing is approved, it may be thought that all books can as well be oversewed by machine, but this is not true. Just as bench sewing (i.e. fold sewing by hand) is employed rather than Smyth Machine sewing when one only, or a few books of a size are to be sewed; for a like reason oversewing by hand instead of by machine is indicated for occasional books. Their size or shape may be unusual, the volumes may consist of several leaf sizes or may include extraneous matter as folded maps or stubs, the inner margins (where the sewing is performed) may be excessively narrow, or some other impelling reason may be present for oversewing by hand.

It is of course important, where manual oversewing is employed, that such oversewing be of an approved character. The use of a stabbing machine, and the adoption of a definite pattern of sewing through the thus stabbed holes, should assure regularity in such sewing, with a desirable uniformity from book to book. But some patterns of such sewing admit of greater flexibility in the completed book than do others; and those patterns which, while firm, are least resistant to book-opening are to be preferred. Before the advent of the oversewing machine, quite a number of library binders evidenced their ingenuity by inventing and patenting patterns of what we now call *hand oversewing*. Some of these sewings were rather complicated and produced an undue tightness in the resulting book back. Several however have proved satisfactory, and patents on all have expired, so that they are available for general use. Our preference is for the stitch originated and patented by an English bookbinder (Holloway), due to the fact that the major portion of each stitch in this sewing lies flat on the surface of the sewed section, whereas in most other patterns the stitches penetrate the sections obliquely and necessarily have a greater tendency to cut the paper. Probably the best known of all hand-oversewings is that developed by the dean of library binders, Cedric Chivers, and this sewing penetrates the sections obliquely.

The depth of oversewing in the leaf (i.e. its maximum distance from the back edge of the leaf) is of prime importance. No oversewing should reach into the section more than three-sixteenths of an inch, and on certain books,—especially if the paper is quite flexible,—that distance may be reduced to one-eighth inch. This means that a reasonable inner margin on every leaf to be oversewed is imperative, and that a liberal width of inner margin is greatly to be preferred. Occasionally books cannot be oversewed because of the inclusion in them of double plates, extra wide printing on certain pages, or even excessive irregularity in width of inner margins. An occasional double plate can be set out (hinged) on a stub through which the sewing will penetrate without perforating the plate. This is possible only where the double plate has front margins of width sufficient for a trim equal to the distance that the plate is set out on the stub.

Thickness of section is also a determining factor in the success of oversewing. It is conceivable that sections may be made too thin so that an excessive amount of thread will be deposited in the back of the book, but this fault is of rare occurrence. The temptation to speed up sewing, and thus reduce cost of production, can lead to making sections excessively thick. This is an inexcusable practice, as it results in inflexible books,—more like stitched than sewed volumes,—and in irregular resistant opening which tempts readers to break the backs of such books. The use of a good mechanical section divider serves to obviate irregular and over-thick sections, such as unaided manual sectioning is sure to produce.

It is to be understood that in preparing books to be oversewed their original sections are generally ignored, due to the fact that their backs are trimmed or "sanded" off sufficiently to reduce all signatures to separate leaves. This is done for two reasons; one is to simplify preparation for oversewing with attendant economy in cost, and the other is to make possible the formation of sections in a thickness best suited to oversewing. The thickness of original signatures in books varies greatly; the correct thickness of sections for oversewing should not vary, and by reducing signatures to individual leaves, then tableting them with glue, and finally dividing them into sections, the thickness can be nicely controlled to assure best results in oversewing.

Oversewing presupposes the use of cloth-guarded end sheets, the exact design of which is of less importance than that the reinforcing shall be equal in strength to good muslin, and that it shall be incorporated in the end sheets and sewed to the book the same as each section is sewed. The reinforcing material may be so placed that it is observable in the finished binding, or it may be hidden under the exposed end sheet. Comparable strength and durability are attainable from either, so that the exposed or the hidden cloth joint is rather a matter of personal choice than of desirability. The reinforcing fabric, of suitable quality and dimensions and sewed to the book as already indicated, performs two most important offices in the rebound book: it protects the joint of the end sheet against parting at the fold, and it affords an important means of attachment between book body and cover. The inexperienced person may have an impulse to criticise the oversewed book for its (usual) lack of tapes and cords, but the experienced person sees in the sewed-on reinforcement of each end sheet in the oversewed book the equivalent of a continuous tape from head to tail of the book. In other words, the fold sewed book (if it has tapes) depends on three or four separate tape ends to attach the book to its board cover, whereas the oversewed book with its continuous sewed-on strip has this to attach the book to its board cover.

Summing up, it is to be remembered that we have modern oversewing (whether by hand or by machine) because we must sew modern book paper. No other book sewing is quite so moderate in cost of production; it is suitable for a very wide range of papers,—especially if scoring be employed on the less flexible; it has great initial strength without straining the paper, hence is suited for long and severe service; it is consequently the sewing commonly specified and generally used by library binders for re-binding most books and for the first binding of usual periodicals. Price schedules for library binding, unless otherwise specified, are based upon the use of oversewing; and variations therefrom which are necessitated because of peculiarities in the material to be sewed, are properly chargeable as "extras."

(4) Oversewing, by machine. What has already been said with reference to preparing material for oversewing by hand,—width of margins, scoring, thickness of sections, type of end sheets,—applies equally to oversewing by machine. The Oversewing Machine was invented during the period between the years 1912 and 1920 and was put onto the market by the writer of this article in the latter year. Since that date all generally recognized library binders of the United States and Canada, besides a number in Scotland and England, have adopted and continue to use the Oversewing Machine. The Government Printing Office (Washington) has several of the machines, including one of extra width for oversewing newspapers; as does also the British Government in its bindery in connection with the British Museum.

It is generally understood that specifications for library binding are based on sewing by means of the Oversewing Machine; however, in order to not hinder any small binder who does not own an Oversewing Machine, the specifications read in effect: "oversewing, by hand or by machine."

It is not to be understood that all users of Oversewing Machines produce uniformly equally good sewing. These machines, just like automobiles or any other equipment subjected to hard service, must be kept in good mechanical condition in order to produce the best of sewing. An automobile is considered old, if not actually worn out, after five years, but there are Oversewing Machines still turning out books after three times that length of time! The desirability of replacement of such machines would seem to be clearly indicated. However faulty sewing is more frequently due to *improper operation* of the machine, and, back of that, to careless preparation of the material to be sewed,—as too thick sections,—rather than to actual machine trouble. All in all, a uniformly high grade of book sewing is turned out by library binders generally year after year on the Oversewing Machine. Those producing defective sewing for any reason whatever are noticeably few in number,—which fact is alike a credit to library binders and to the machine on which they oversew most of their books and periodicals.

In conclusion: This article has attempted to draw a distinction between *book stitching* and *book sewing* (terms already recognized by Webster's Unabridged Dictionary), and to encourage a more discriminating use of these terms. It has pointed out that book stitching *through the central fold* may be dismissed with brief consideration because it is a method impossible of use on any but very thin books, really pamphlets. The article has drawn further attention to the physical handicaps of side-stitched books, so common in the field of school texts, and has pointed out that the machines which produce such work, though called "sewing" machines, are in fact really book *stitching machines*. The principal valid claim of such stitching machines, contrary to some of their advertising misconceptions, is solely to cheapness of production, and in no sense to excellence of product from a bookbinding standpoint.

Finally this article has attempted to present the fundamentals of *real book sewing,* both that done through the folds of sections and that done through the edges of sections, alike as performed by hand and by machine in each case. When looking at book sewing idealistically, the ancient craft *bench sewing* was necessarily revered, but when looking at the subject practically, modern book sewing machines had to be commended for sewing most publishers' books, while the Oversewing Machine, supplemented by occasional hand oversewing, had to be accredited alone for the field of library binding.

APPENDIX 4

Hearings before the Sub-Committee on Antitrust and Monopoly of the Committee on the Judiciary, U.S. Senate, 89th Congress, Second Session, U.S. Government Printing Office, 1966. Letter from Harry N. Peterson and Maxine LaBounty to Dan Lacy, April 2, 1965. Letter from Dudley A. Weiss to Harry N. Peterson, April 19, 1965.

Mr. Dan Lacy, Managing Director
American Book Publishers Council, Inc.
58 West 40th Street
New York, New York 10018

Dear Mr. Lacy:

At the midwinter meeting of the directors of the nineteen largest public libraries in the United States and Canada held this year in Washington, D. C., on January 27, the discussion centered on the problems related to publishers' reinforced bindings sold to libraries at net prices.

Expressions of mutual concern were voiced on the following points:

1. *The inferior quality of many publishers' reinforced bindings.*
   The bindings of many library editions are unsatisfactory and unsuitable for public libraries. Furthermore, there is a lack of uniformity in what is supplied as a publishers' reinforced binding. In this connection it is noted that the American Library Association has not yet issued its criteria for standards of reinforced bindings as differentiated from trade bindings or Class A prebindings.

2. *Net pricing.*
   The publishers' and jobbers' practice of net pricing library editions seriously reduces the number of children's books which can be purchased by a given library. No discounts are allowed for quantity buying. Furthermore, the quality of publishers' reinforced bindings in no way justifies the price differential.

3. *Unavailability of trade editions or sheets for prebinding.*
   It is acknowledged that in the case of picture books, flats and oversized books, there is need for a binding which is less sturdy than a prebind but stronger than a trade edition. However, for many other books, such as titles for older children and young adults, the trade editions are preferred. For still others the prebinds have proven more satisfactory and less expensive. However, in many instances

neither the trade edition nor sheets for prebinding are available. Consequently, in some instances, where the library edition is the only edition available, children's librarians have considered that they have no alternative but to drop the title from their replacement lists.

It is recognized that publishers and book dealers must charge prices which will insure reasonable profits. On the other hand, librarians have the responsibility for spending book appropriations wisely and economically, and they note with deep concern that with each passing year a larger percentage of children's titles are available only in publishers' reinforced bindings—at net price.

Expressions of dissatisfaction by individual librarians have had little effect. For this reason, the library directors and heads of children's work who are listed in the attached sheet have taken this means of expressing their common concern to responsible publishing organizations.

It would appear that there is need for more adequate communications between publishers and librarians to discuss the topics mentioned above. A large meeting would not seem advisable, but we should like to suggest that a few representatives of publishing houses and the directors of some of the largest public libraries meet together for this purpose. We should like to suggest further that you make known to your members our dissatisfaction with the present situation as regards publisher's reinforced editions and our earnest wish to find a mutually satisfactory solution.

As convener of the meeting in Washington, I should appreciate hearing from you and receiving your suggestions for setting up a suitable meeting.

Sincerely yours,

Harry N. Peterson, Director
Public Library of the District of Columbia

Maxine LaBounty, Coordinator
Children's Service
Public Library of the District of Columbia

HEADS OF CHILDREN'S WORK OF LARGE LIBRARIES

Name of Library	Heads of Children's Work
Boston Public Library	Miss Ruth Marie Hayes, Coord., Children's Service
Brooklyn Public Library	Miss Harriet B. Quimby, Coord., Children's Service
Buffalo and Erie County Public Library	Miss Lucille Adams, Coord., Children's Work
Carnegie Library	Miss Virginia Chase, Head Boys and Girls Department
Chicago Public Library	Miss Marie C. Will, Supvr. of Work with Children-Cent. Lib.

Name of Library	*Heads of Children's Work*
Cincinnati and Hamilton County Public Library	Miss Jane Ann McGregor, Supvr., Work with Children
Cleveland Public Library	Miss Adeline Corrigan, Supvr., Work with Children
Detroit Public Library	Miss Marian C. Young, Coord., Children's Service
D. C. Public Library	Miss Maxine LaBounty, Coord., Children's Service
Enoch Pratt Free Library	Miss Isabella Jinnette, Coord., Work with Children
Los Angeles County Public Library	Mrs. Carmen Collier, Coord., Children's Services
Los Angeles Public Library	Miss Rosemary E. Livsey, Coord., Children's Services
Milwaukee Public Library	Miss Mary Elizabeth Ledlie, Coord., Work with Youth
New York Public Library	Mrs. Augusta Baker, Coord., Children's Service
Philadelphia Free Library	Mrs. Carolyn Wicker Field, Coord., Work with Children
Queens Borough Public Library	Mrs. Ellen A. Pryor, Children's Librarian
San Francisco Public Library	Miss Effie Lee Morris, Coord., Children's Library Activities
St. Louis Public Library	Miss Leone F. Garvey, Supvr., Children's Department
Toronto Public Library Canada	Miss Marguerite G. Bagshaw, Head of Boys and Girls Services

April 19, 1965
Mr. Harry N. Peterson, Director
Public Library,
District of Columbia,
Washington, D. C.

Dear Mr. Peterson:

We are in receipt of a copy of your letter, dated April 2, sent to Mr. Dan Lacy pertaining to publishers' reinforced bindings.

For many years, Library Binding Institute has taken a position comparable in many ways to that voiced by your committee. It can be summed up as follows:

1. There is a standard for prebound library books. In 1939 these were issued under the title "Standards for Reinforced (Pre-Library Bound) New Books" and were approved by Council of American Library Association, the Library Binding Institute, and the Book Buying Committee of American Library Association. They were an adaptation of the "Minimum Specifications for Class A Library

Binding of the American Library Association and Library Binding Institute" issued in 1935. Subsequently, they were issued by Library Binding Institute with the Class A specifications in the present "Library Binding Institute Standard for Library Binding."

2. Libraries may need many types of volumes in their collections, including trade editions, reinforced editions, and library bound editions; but in every case, they are entitled to know what they are buying. Many publishers advertise their editions as library binding, which is false and misleading, for the volumes do not conform to specifications for library binding. They are mostly adaptations of textbook specifications. The Commercial Standard for Cover Material used until very recently in textbook specifications clearly and specifically stated that such materials were not to be used in library binding. The loose and inaccurate use of terminology is misleading, to say the least, and is a misrepresentation proscribed by law and specifically included in the FTC's Trade Practice Rules for the Library Binding Industry.

3. The guarantees and other claims made for many reinforced editions do not in many cases protect libraries. For example, our members rebind thousands of textbooks and reinforced editions where the paper long outlasts the covers. Such guarantees of performance are meaningless as a practical matter for librarians to enforce. The present situation is comparable to what existed in rebinding prior to the issuance of specifications for methods and materials.

4. The practices with respect to net pricing and restricting availability of trade editions or sheets for prebinding does not enlarge the publisher's market, but reduces it for the reasons stated by you and, therefore reduces rather than increases publishers' profits. Yet libraries are limited in the number of volumes they can acquire. Whether a publisher sells to a library or to a prebinder does not enlarge his market. The library should have a choice to buy from either, depending upon the character of the binding it wants. In either event the publisher sells the volume. But the library can acquire the type of binding it thinks meets its end use needs. It would seem to the publishers' advantage, as well as that of the library, to make books available in a format so that libraries can purchase them in the type of binding they need.

We have written and published many articles on this subject for THE LIBRARY BINDER and have called this situation to the attention of American Library Association and the Library Technology Project, and welcome your forthright attack upon the problem. Many publishers to whom we have called attention to their advertising have changed their representations. Others have not. We hope your action will produce results. With such a large allocation of national funds being expended on books, great care must be taken to insure that the funds are wisely spent.

We suggest that it would be to the advantage of librarians to have a prebinder present at the proposed meeting in Washington. We will make one available upon your request.

Very truly yours,

(s) Dudley A. Weiss, Executive Director

DAW:cac

APPENDIX 5

TERMS RELATING TO LIBRARY BINDING, INCLUDING TERMS USED IN LIBRARY BINDING MANUAL

Acid Migration—The transfer of acid from an acid material, such as pulp paper, to a less-acid material when the two are stored in contact with one another. The transfer will usually cause weakening and staining of the less-acid materials. Also referred to as Acid Transfer.

Adhesive Binding—See Perfect Binding

All Along—In hand sewing of books, with the thread passing from kettle stitch to kettle stitch of successive sections, one complete course of thread going to each section. Also called One Sheet On and One On.

Alum-Tawed Leather—Leather (usually pigskin) treated with alum instead of a tanbark or other tanning agents. The surface resembles a vellum in its consistency, except for the additional pigskin pores. This type of binding is often found on books bound from the twelfth century through the Renaissance and they have demonstrated great durability and permanence.

Art Book—Any volume, on art or related subjects, which contains many illustrations (particularly in plate form), requiring mounting, sewing through the folds, or other special care in binding.

Artificial Gold—See Imitation Gold

Artificial Leather—A term used for chemically coated fabrics made to resemble leather, especially in the graining.

Artist Binder—A binder using the medium of the bookbinding as a work of art.

Back—1. The combined back edges of a bound volume, as secured together and shaped in binding. (Not to be confused with Backbone, Backstrip, Shelf Back or Spine) (q. v.), 2. The endmost leaves of a volume, usually devoted to the index, appendices and the like.

Back or Backing—To shape a ridge on each side of the back of a sewed volume, prior to covering, by way of compensation for the thickness of the boards, and to provide a hinge-line for the cover to swing from without strain.

Back Cover—That part of the book cover following the endmost leaves.

Back Edge—The left-hand edge of a recto, corresponding to the right-hand edge of a verso. This is the binding edge in the case of the ordinary bound volume.

Back Lining—1. Generally, the materials (paper or fabric) used to line the back of a book prior to encasing it in a loose back (or hollow back) cover. Specifically, in Class "A" library binding, this must be Canton flannel, in edition binding, crash or crash and paper are used. 2. The muslin reinforcement on the back of some papercovered books. 3. Sometimes in library binding, the paper used for stiffening the back-bone of the cover. (The preferred term for this is Inlay.)

Back Margin—The left-hand margin of a printed recto and the right-hand margin of a printed verso. In the ordinary book, the back mar-gin adjoins the binding edge.

Backbone—That portion of a bound volume which stands exposed when ranged with others on the shelf, cover to cover, in the usual way. Also called Spine and Shelf Back.

Backing—See Rounding and Backing

Backing Boards—Bevelled hardwood boards used in connection with a press for backing volumes in lieu of the more generally used job-backer with its bevelled steel jaws.

Backing Hammer—A hammer with a short handle and a flat, broad face, used in rounding and backing.

Backing Machine—A machine for backing books. See Round and Back.

Backstrip—1. The Spine (q. v.) of a book. Sometimes called Back. 2. That portion of a cover material which extends from joint to joint. 3. Erroneous usage for Inlay (q. v.).

Bands—1. The cords or tapes on which the sections of a book are sewed, when not let into prepared saw-cuts across the back. 2. The ridges across the backbone of certain leather-bound volumes. 3. Loosely, gold-creased lines across the backbone of a volume.

Barrier Sheets—Pieces of paper used as barriers to prevent migration of acid or oil from one material to another.

Belt—The uncut fold of paper at the head, fore edge, and foot of a signature.

Bench Sewing—Sewing through the folds, by hand, on the sewing bench; suspended cords (or tapes) to which the sections are to be sewed, are arranged across the back edges of the sections.

Bind "As Is"—A direction to the binder to bind material in the order or in the condition in which it is submitted by the customer, regard-less of any seeming imperfection.

Bind In—To fasten securely into the binding; said of any supple-mentary material.

Binder's Board—A high-quality, single-ply, solid pulp board for book-binding, made to full thickness in one operation, from mixed papers, and kiln-dried or plate-dried. Sometimes called Millboard.

Bindery Slip—See Binding Slip

Binding—1. The process of producing a single volume from leaves, sheets, signatures, or issues of periodicals, or of covering such a vol-ume. 2. The finished work produced by this process. 3. The cover of a volume.

Binding Edge—The edge of a volume (usually the back edge) that is to receive the main binding treatment (sewing, rounding-and-back-ing, etc.).

Binding Slip—A sheet (large or small) of instructions sent to the bindery with each volume, specifying the binding requirements for that particular volume.

Bleed—In binding, to trim printed matter so that the text or illustration is cut into.

Bleed Illustration—An illustration printed so as to run to the extreme edge of the page, leaving no margin.

Board—The binder's board, pasted board, chip board, news board, and laminated board used as a foundation for book covers. So called because wood was originally used.

Board Paper—See Paste-down

Boards—A form of bookbinding in which the boards are covered with paper. Also called Paper Boards.

Book—From the bindery point of view, any number of leaves in a binding or to be bound. Cf. Magazine. Also, any collection of more than 64 pages, bound in any manner or material. Cf. Pamphlet.

Book Jacket—A detachable wrapper, plain or printed, flush with the covers of head and tail, but folded over between the cover (both front and back) and the book proper. Also called Dust Cover, Dust Jacket, Dust Wrapper, Jacket, Jacket Cover and Wrapper.

Bookbinding—See Binding

Bookplate—An owner's identification label, usually with a distinct design, pasted to the inside cover of a book, also called Ex Libris.

Bosses—Brass or other metal knobs attached to the boards of books for ornamental or protective purposes.

Bound In—See Bind In

Brass-Bound Boards—Wooden boards edged with a brass strip projecting beyond the face of the board, used by binders for defining the groove in a case binding; also called brass-edged boards.

Brayer—A printer's hand inking roller.

Break—A parting of adjacent sections due to loosening of the sewing.

Bristol Board—A thin paperboard with a smooth surface suitable for writing or printing. Index cards are made of bristol board.

Broken—1. Of a book, tending to open readily at a place or places where the binding has been forced or strained. 2. Of a leaf, folded over.

Buckle—To warp and twist in several directions. Said of boards and folded signatures.

Buckram—A filled book cloth with a heavy-weave cotton base. Originally applied only to a starch-filled fabric of this type; now, also, an impregnated fabric with a heavy base.

Bulk—The thickness of a book between its covers.

C Clamp—A c-shaped clamp that clamps between the open ends of the "C" by means of a long screw that passes through one end of the "C" and presses against the clamped material.

Call Mark—See Call Number

Call Number—Letters, figures, and symbols, separate or in combination, assigned to a book to indicate its location on shelves. It usually consists of class number and book number. Sometimes known as Call Mark or Shelf Number.

Cancel—Any part of a book (a leaf or leaves) intended to be substituted for the corresponding part of the book as originally printed.

Canton Flannel—A soft cotton fabric with a nap on one side; used as back lining material in library binding.

Case—A cover that is made complete before it is affixed to a volume.

Case Binding—A method of binding in which the book covers are made separate from the book and later attached to it; distinguished from those methods in which the cover cannot be constructed as a separate unit. Sometimes called Casework.

Casework—See Case Binding

Casing-in—The process of putting a volume that has received all of the binding or rebinding operations into its cover or case.

Cellulose Acetate Film Lamination—See Lamination

Certified Bindery—A library bindery which has been approved as qualifying under the Certification Plan of the Library Binding Institute.

Chain Stitch—See Kettle Stitch

Clasp—A hinged catch for holding together the covers of a book being bound.

Cloth Binding—A book bound in full, half, or quarter cloth.

Cloth Sides—Having cloth as the side material of the covers of a volume, as in half, quarter, and three-quarter binding.

Coil Binding—See Spiral Binding

Collate—In library binding, to examine a book or magazine volume, page by page, before binding, in order to determine completeness and nature of material, to diagnose material, sewing, and other treatment, and to arrange material in proper sequence, preparatory to sewing.

Combination Press—A press that combines the functions of a number of presses. For instance, a press that serves as a standing press, backing press and a casing-in press.

Compensation Guards—Short stubs bound in a volume to balance the space taken up by bulky inserts.

Concealed Joint—See Invisible Joint

Cords—Heavy hemp, cotton, or linen strings to which sections are sewed in the process of binding a book by hand. Cf. Tapes and Bands.

Corner—1. The junction point of two edges of a book cover (usually the outer ones). Various types are: Square Corners, Round Corners, Library Corners, Dutch Corners, and Mitered Corners. (q. v.). 2. The leather or other material on the corners of book covers in half binding and three-quarter binding.

Cover—1. The outer covering of a volume, no matter what material may be employed. 2. Popularly, either of the two side pieces of a cover paper; as, front cover, back cover.

Crash—1. Coarse, open-weave, starched cotton goods, used in edition binding for reinforcing backs of volumes. Also called Super and Gauze. 2. A pattern peculiar to buckram grades of book cloth, showing a coarse pebbled effect.

Cut—1. To trim the edges of a book. 2. Of a book, having cut edges. Not to be confused with Opened (q. v.).

Cut Flush—Of a bound volume, having the cover trimmed after binding, so that its edges are even with the edges of the leaves. Also called Trimmed Flush.

Deckle Edge—The rough, feathery edge of handmade paper, caused by a frame called the "deckle" used in molding the paper; or a similar edge in machine-made paper. Also called Feathered Edge.

Decorated Covers—In library binding, bindings in which the front cover, and sometimes the spine, has an illustration, design or special lettering.

Dog-eared—Having leaves turned down at the corners, or corners of covers broken.

Dust Cover—See Book Jacket

Dust Jacket—See Book Jacket

Dutch Corner—See Library Corner

Edition Binding—The kind of bookbinding that is furnished to the book trade, i.e., quantity binding in uniform style for a large number of copies of single titles. Cf. Publishers' Binding.

End-Leaf—See End Papers

End Papers—(Front and Back). That part of the front and back of each library bound volume which attaches the volume to its cover. By LBI Standard, end papers shall consist of three functional parts: a pasted-down or outward end-leaf which becomes the cover lining, at least two free fly-leaves, and reinforcing fabric.

End Sheet—See End Papers

Ex-Libris—See Bookplate

Extra Binding—The binding of books with more than ordinary care and handling and/or with a higher quality of material, usually with ornamentation. Generally binding in leather, but formerly binding done by hand as distinguished from case binding.

Fabrikoid—The trade name for a brand of pyroxylin-coated cloth. The term is sometimes used generically.

Feathered Edge—See Deckle Edge

Felt Pads—Pieces of binder's board covered on both sides with felt.

Fiber Cover—An extra-stiff but slightly flexible cover stock, used on large sized pamphlet-like material.

Filled—Treated with a chemical compound which fills the interstices and/or covers the fibers of a fabric, to give it body, color, or other physical or chemical properties.

Filler—The blank pages added at the back of a thin pamphlet when it is bound as a sizable volume. Also called Padding.

Filler—(2) The material used to fill the interstices of a fabric, i.e., starch, china clay, pyroxylin or other non-fibrous materials.

Filling—The threads that run crosswise of the fabric from selvage to selvage.

Fine Binding—A valuable or rare book bound in a special manner. Distinguished from books bound in the regular library binding. Usually incorporating the techniques of the artist binder.

Finisher—The person who does the lettering and/or ornamentation on book bindings.

Flag—A marker placed to protrude from the leaves of a book to show a special position or to indicate that special attention should be given either to the book or the page marked.

Flange—See Ridge

Flat Back—A book back that is at right angles with the sides; opposed to the usual round back.

Flat Sewing—See Side Stitching

Flat Stitching—See Side Stitching

Flexible Binding—1. Any binding having other material than stiff boards in its cover. 2. Any binding that permits the book to open perfectly flat.

Flexible Glue—An adhesive made of a mixture of glue and some material like glycerine, to keep it from becoming dry and brittle.

Flush—See Cut Flush

Fly-Leaf—1. A blank leaf at the beginning or the end of a volume, between the lining paper and the first or last section. 2. Loosely, also the blank free half of a lining paper or a blank leaf which is part of the first or last section.

Foil—Leaf used in stamping lettering in imitation gold, silver, or other colors.

Fold—A bend in any flexible material, such as paper, made by turning a sheet over upon itself.

Fold Sewing—The process of sewing through the central (or binding) fold of section after section of a volume by hand or machine. Also called Sewing Through the Fold.

Folder—A piece of bone, shaped like a knife blade, used for folding sheets of paper or other material.

Folio Recto—See Recto

Folio Verso—See Verso

Fore Edge—The front or outer edge of a book. Also called Front Edge.

Forwarding—In extra, job and library binding, the group of operations that follow the sewing, except those having to do with lettering and finishing the cover. They include trimming, backing, etc., lining up, headbanding and covering.

Foxing—The discoloration of paper by dull rusty patches, variously attributed to fungus, impurities in manufacture, sulphur dioxide in the atmosphere and dampness.

Front Cover—That portion of a book cover in front of the foremost leaves.

Front Edge—See Fore Edge

Full Binding—The binding of a book completely (both back and sides) with any one material. Strictly speaking, this term and also the term Full Bound, should apply only to leather bindings. Also called Whole Binding. See also Half Binding, Quarter Binding and Three-Quarter Binding.

Gauze—See Crash

Gilt Edge—Book edges that have been covered with gold leaf and burnished.

Glassine Paper—A thin, dense translucent paper which is resistant to the passage of air and dirt.

Glue Off—1. To apply glue (flexible glue, in library binding) to the binding edge of a volume, after the other three edges have been trimmed, and just prior to backing (or rounding and backing). 2. Formerly to apply glue, by hand, to cloth, paper or leather in cover making.

Gold—Short for Gold Leaf (q. v.).

Gold Leaf—Genuine gold, beaten into a thin leaf, adapted for use in lettering.

Grain—1. In leather, the markings on the outer surface, after the hair has been removed. 2. In paper and binder's board, the direction in which the fibers of a sheet generally lie. 3. The artificially embossed surface of leather or other material.

Groove—1. A depression along each side of the back of a volume, formed during the process of rounding and backing. 2. A depression along the binding edge of front and back covers. 3. The space between the board and the back of the volume in an open joint.

Guard—1. A strip of paper, muslin, or other thin material on which an insert, leaf, section or map may be fastened to permit free bending.

Also called Stub. 2. Strips of paper or fabric put together to act as a guard and also to equalize the space to be taken up by a folded insert. 3. A strip of paper or other material reinforcing a signature.

Guarded Signatures or Sections—Signatures or sections, usually the first and the last of a volume, that have paper or other reinforcing material pasted around the back (fold) to condition them for sewing.

Gutter—The combined marginal space formed by the two inner margins of facing pages of a volume.

Half Binding—A style of binding having a leather back and leather corners, and cloth or paper sides. The leather of the back should extend onto the boards one-quarter the width of the board, and the corners should be in harmonious proportion. The term Half Binding is applied also to any similar combination of two different materials.

Hard Cover—Stiff board covers.

Head—1. The top of a volume or page. 2. By extension, the top portion of the backbone of a bound volume.

Headband—A small ornamented band (sometimes protective), generally of mercerized cotton or silk, placed at the head and tail of a volume between the cover and the backs of the folded signatures or sections. (Formerly the two were distinguished as Headband and Tailband; now both are called Headbands.)

Headcap—The covering material that has been shaped over the headbands at the head and foot of the backbone of a book.

Height—Length of cover from head to tail of volume.

Hinge—Any paper or muslin stub or guard that permits the free turning of an insert, leaf, section or map.

Hollow Back—See Loose Back

Illustrated Covers—In library binding, bindings in which the front cover has a decoration embodying an approximate reproduction of the design on the original publisher's cover or book jacket.

Imitation Cloth—Paper which has been embossed to give it the surface appearance of a fabric.

Imitation Gold—A metallic composition, much used as a substitute for genuine gold leaf on book covers. Also called Artificial Gold.

Impregnated—A term inaccurately used for Filled in the case of pyroxylin-filled fabric, since the filling compound does not penetrate the fibers of the fabric.

Imprint—1. The name of the owner of a book as stamped on the binding (usually at tail of spine). 2. The name of the publisher as stamped on the publisher's binding (usually at the tail of the spine).

Inlay—In library binding, the paper used for stiffening, the backbone of the cover. Commonly, but erroneously, called Back Lining or Backstrip.

Insert—1. An illustration, map, or other piece produced separately from the body of the book, but bound in it. 2. In newspapers and magazines, and sometimes other publications, an extraneous piece, not originally an integral part of the publication, slipped in to accompany the publication.

Inside Margin—1. The part of the turn-in on a book cover not covered by the end paper. 2. The Back Margin (q. v.).

Inside Strip—See Joint

Interleaf—An extra leaf, usually blank, bound in between any two regular leaves of a volume, to provide space for writing or to protect pictures.

Invisible Joint—A cloth book joint of reinforcing fabric so made that it cannot be seen in the finished book. Sometimes called Concealed Joint.
Issue—(of a periodical)—See Number
Jacket—See Book Jacket
Jacket Cover—See Book Jacket
Japanese Tissue—A very thin, strong, transparent tissue paper, often pasted on each side of old or worn paper to preserve it. Used also for mending tears in paper. (Strictly speaking, the term refers to such paper made only in Japan, but it applies also to a similar paper made in the United States.)
Job Backer—A machine used for backing a book by hand.
Joint—1. Either of the two portions of the covering material that bend at the groove and along the flange when the covers of a bound volume are opened or closed. Sometimes called Inside Strip or Hinge. 2. (pl.) The reinforcements applied to the end linings or to the combination of end papers and end sections, designed to strengthen the binding.
Kettle Stitch—A stitch used in book sewing, by means of which each section is firmly united to the preceding one at head and tail. Also called the Chain Stitch.
Kraft—A tough, strong paper, made entirely from wood pulp produced by a modified sulphate pulping process.
Label—A piece of paper or other material, printed or stamped, affixed to the cover of a volume. The usual position is on the spine or front cover.
Lamination—The fusing of sheets of protective film to one or both sides of a piece of deacidified (or undeacidified) paper by means of heat and pressure. Tissue or other strong material is frequently applied to the outer surfaces of the plastic film to increase the strength of the lamination. Also called: Archival Lamination or Cellulose Acetate Film Lamination.
Leaf—1. One of the units into which the original sheet or half sheet of paper, parchment, etc. is folded or divided to form a book. A leaf consists of two pages, one on each side, either or both of which may be blank, or may bear printing, writing or illustration. 2. Gold leaf. 3. Thin metallic sheets, other than gold, used in lettering.
Legal Buckram—Trade name for a heavy starch-filled buckram.
Less-Used Materials Specifications—Designation by librarians for the application of binding other than "library binding to certain materials." Also known as LUMSPECS.
Lettering—The process or result of marking a cover with the title or other distinguishing characters (and, loosely, accompanying ornamentation).
Library Binding—1. Volumes bound according to the LBI Standard for Library Binding whether rebinding of new or used volumes, prebinding of new volumes (also called prebounds, prebinds, pre-library bound), and binding of periodicals, as distinguished from publishers' edition binding, library edition, or other binding not in accordance with this standard. This special form of bookbinding is designed for strength and durability to withstand severe library use. 2. The process employed in producing such a binding.
Library Buckram—1. A heavy weight cotton fabric having the qualities called for in the Minimum Specifications for Class "A" Library Binding. 2. A trade name sometimes erroneously applied to all cloths of a similar nature.

Library Corner—A book corner in which the covering material is not cut, the excess being taken up in two diagonal folds, one under each turn-in. Also called Dutch Corner, Round Corner.

Line Up or Lining Up—In library binding, to strengthen a volume (after sewing, trimming and, usually, backing) by applying glue to the back and affixing the flannel and any reinforcing material.

Linen—1. A book cloth made of flax. 2. A book cloth made of cotton in imitation of genuine linen. 3. A book cloth pattern that resembles the texture of linen.

Lining Paper—1. A strong paper used for the end papers of a volume. 2. The end papers themselves. 3. The paper used for lining the backs of heavy books, supplementing the lining fabric.

Lining Strip—See Inlay

Lithographic Stone—A fine-grained dense slab of limestone prepared for lithography but used by bookbinders as a surface on which to pare leather or for other purposes where a flat stone is called for.

Lock Stitch—See Kettle Stitch

Loose Back—The back of a book in which the covering material is not glued to the back. Also called Hollow Back, Open Back, Spring Back.

Magazine—A publication with a distinctive title, intended to appear in successive (usually unbound) numbers or parts at stated or regular intervals and, as a rule, for an indefinite time. Each number or part generally contains articles by several contributors.

Margin—The space on a page outside the printed or written matter. The four margins are commonly designated as: Head or top; fore edge, outer or outside; tail or bottom; back, inner, inside or gutter.

Matching—Reasonably approximate duplication, as to lettering, cover material, paper, etc.

Mending—Minor restoration, not involving replacement with any new material or the separation of book from cover.

Millboard—See Binder's Board

Mitered Corner—A book corner in which a triangular piece of the covering material is cut off at the corner so that the turn-ins meet without overlapping.

Monograph—For library binding purposes: A separate treatise or thesis on a single subject; when two or more are bound together, a periodical.

Mull—See Super

Nap—The loose fibers attached to the surface of a fabric.

Newsprint—Cheap paper made largely from wood pulp, on which newspapers are printed.

Number—(Publication) A single numbered or dated issue of a series, a magazine, or a serial publication; generally so slight in extent that two or more may be bound together to form a volume.

Offset—Unintentional transfer of ink (usually from the surface of a freshly printed sheet to the back of a sheet placed on top of it); also the ink or image transferred by the above process; also called set off.

One On—See All Along

One Sheet On—See All Along

Open Back—See Loose Back

Open-Back Case—See Slipcase

Opened—Of a book in which the folds of the sheets have been slit open so as to separate the leaves for reading. Not to be confused with Cut (q. v.).

Ordinary Book Volume—Any ordinary sized graphic material consisting of an appreciable number of leaves or folded sheets produced originally as a unit and submitted for binding, rebinding or pre-binding as such a unit and not requiring special handling.

Ordinary Periodical Volume—A series of multileaved, like-constituted, serially numbered graphic units submitted for binding or rebinding into a scheduled multi-unit volume and not requiring special handling.

Overcasting—Hand sewing in which each section is sewn through and over the binding edge. (In older usage, a generic term, including oversewing and whipstitching.)

Oversewing—Sewing, by hand or machine, through the edge of each section in consecutive order, using preformed holes through which the needle passes.

Padding—See Filler

Page—The single side of a leaf of a book.

Pamphlet—From the bindery point of view, a pamphlet is any collection of leaves, paper bound or self-covered, consisting of 64 pages or less.

Pamphlet Binding—1. Binding done by a printer or for a printer, in which the sheets, as they come from the press, are wire-stitched. The term applies both to pamphlets and to magazines. 2. The manner in which pamphlets and magazines are bound as they come from the publisher; usually wire-stitched, either side-stitched or saddle-stitched.

Pamphlet-style Library Binding—A style of binding for a pamphlet or a thin group of pamphlets and magazines are bound as they come from the publisher; usually wire-stitched, either side-stitched or saddle-stitched.

Pamphlet-style Library Binding—A style of binding for a pamphlet or a thin group of pamphlets when use is expected to be infrequent. Its characteristics are side-stitching, usually with wire, and covers with cloth hinges, usually of plain boards, heavy paper, paper-covered boards or thin lightweight cloth, cut flush, without gold lettering. (This style should not be confused with Class "A" library binding, as no process or material is of Class "A" standard).

Paper-backed—See Paper-bound

Paper Boards—See Boards

Paper-bound—Bound simply with a paper cover. Also called Paper-backed.

Parchment—A skin prepared with lime and not tanned like leather.

Paste-down—That half of the lining paper which is pasted to the inner face of the cover. Also called Board Paper.

Pattern—In binding magazines, and the like, a sample volume, sample back, rub-off, and/or other data used for matching the style.

Perfect Binding—1. A type of binding in which single leaves are kept together by adhesive which joins them to the backbone. The covers are usually paper. 2. The process employed in producing such a binding. Sometimes called Adhesive Binding.

Periodical—See Magazine

Perma-film—Self-adhering and transparent material used for covering and protection of pages.

Pickup-cards—Cards left by the binder when he picks up book for binding.

Plastic Covers—See Jacket cover

Plastic Binding—A type of flat-opening binding used for pamphlets, commercial catalogs, etc. The single leaves and the separate front and back covers are fastened by means of a specially cut piece of synthetic plastic having prongs (combs) that pass through slots near the binding edge and are curled back within the cylinder thus formed by the plastic.

Plate—A full-page illustration on a leaf which normally is blank on the other side. The reverse may, however, bear a descriptive legend, the title of the work, or another plate. The leaf is usually of special (heavy) paper and may or may not be included in the pagination.

Portfolio—A case for holding loose papers, engravings, or similar material, consisting of two covers joined together at the back and usually tied at the front and the ends.

Prebinding (also called prebounds, prebinds)—Short for pre-library binding (pre-library-bound). 1. New volumes bound according to LBI Standard for Library Binding as distinguished from publishers' edition binding, library edition, or other binding not in accordance with this Standard. 2. The process used in producing binding according to this Standard.

Prebound—Short for Pre-library-bound (q. v.).

Pre-library Binding—See Prebinding

Pre-library-Bound—Of new books, bound in library binding prior to or at the time of original sale.

Protective Container—A slipcase, box, solander case, or portfolio designed to contain and protect a book, pamphlet or manuscript.

Publisher's Binding—The binding of a book as it is issued by its publisher. It is nearly always identical with edition binding, and commonly implies ordinary cloth.

Publisher's Cover—A case designed for use in an edition binding.

Pulp Paper—Paper with a high pulp-wood content.

Pyroxylin-coated—Referring to a fabric completely and heavily covered with a nitro-cellulose compound. (Loosely applied to fabrics with cellulose acetate coating.)

Pyroxylin-filled—Referring to a fabric filled but not heavily covered with a nitro-cellulose compound. (Loosely applied to fabrics with cellulose acetate filling.) Frequently called Pyroxylin Impregnated, although the word Impregnated is not strictly accurate.

Pyroxylin Impregnated—See Pyroxylin-filled

Quarter Binding—Binding in cloth-covered boards, with leather backs (or paper-covered sides, with cloth or leather backs), in which the back material extends only slightly onto the sides. In quarter binding, the leather (or cloth) back should extend one-eighth the width of the boards onto those boards.

Rag Paper—Paper with a high rag (cotton, silk) content.

Rebinding—The thorough rehabilitation of a worn volume, the minimum of work done being resewing and, if necessary, putting on a new cover.

Reconstructed Binding—Trade name for a pre-library binding on a new book.

Recto—The right-hand page of an open book, usually bearing the odd page number. Also, the front of a separate printed sheet, e.g. of a broadside. Formerly called Folio Recto.

Reinforced Binding—1. Term loosely used by publishers for edition bindings which purport to be strengthened sufficiently to withstand hard library use. 2. Inadequate term for pre-library binding. See Pre-library-bound.

Reinforced Library Binding—A secondary binding in pre-library-bound style. Properly used only to refer to Class "A" pre-library binding, but sometimes used in referring to a prebound book in which the publisher's original cover is retained.

Reinforcing—Strengthening the structure of a weakened volume, usually by adding material. (For example, the strengthening of a hinge with cloth or the reinforcing of a page by covering it with tissue.)

Reinforcing Fabric—A fabric used for strengthening the end papers at their hinge.

Repairing—The partial rehabilitation of a worn book, the amount of work done being less than the minimum involved in rebinding and more than the maximum involved in mending. Includes such operations as restoring cover and restoring lost corners of leaves.

Reprint—Reproduction in print of matter already printed.

Ridge—Either of the two outer projections along the sides of a backed and rounded volume, against which the cover boards are fitted. Sometimes called Flange or Shoulder.

Rough Edges—A generic term, including Uncut (Untrimmed) Edges and Deckle Edges.

Round—To form the convex back and corresponding concave front in rounding and backing.

Round Back or Rounded Back—A book back that has been given a convex form by rounding and backing.

Round Corner or Rounded Corner—1. Same as Library Corner (q. v.) 2. A book cover in which the board is cut off at the corner before covering; usually confined to leather bindings.

Rounding-and-Backing—The combined operation of rounding and backing a book, to shape it preparatory to covering. See Round and Back.

Rub-off—An impression of the lettering and its position on the backbone of a book, made by placing a piece of strong, thin paper, the exact length of the book and a little wider, over the backbone, exactly even with the bottom of the backbone, and rubbing it with the lead of a heavy pencil or something similar; used for matching bindings. Also called Rubbing.

Rubbing—See Rub-off

Rush—Material to be given special quick binding treatment.

Saddle Stitching—Stitching together leaves (double leaves inserted one within the other) with thread or wire passing through the bulk of the volume at the fold line. So called from the saddle of a stitching machine. Cf. Side Stitching.

Sample Back—A strip of binding material made up like the backstrip of a volume, to be used as a sample for matching color, fabric, lettering, etc.

Sand or Sanding—To clean the edges of a volume by hand, with sandpaper or by a sand-wheel machine, removing the least possible amount of margin from the volume.

Saw Cuts—Grooves in the back of a book made with a saw, for receiving the cords.

Scalpel—A small, straight knife with a thin blade used especially for fine cutting.

Score or Scoring—In library binding, to make a crease near the edge of a section or leaf, in the case of moderately stiff paper, in order to facilitate easy opening of the volume.

Section—1. In library binding, a group of leaves of a volume, suitable for sewing. 2. In Class "A" library binding, a group of leaves of a volume, not exceeding .050 inch in thickness, except flexible pulpy paper, which may not exceed .060 inch each.

Serial—A publication issued in successive parts, usually at regular intervals, and, as a rule, intended to be continued indefinitely.

Set Out—To attach an insert to a guard so that it stands out from the bound back or gutter.

Setoff—See Offset

Sewing—In bookbinding, fastening sections together by means of needle and thread, one at a time, until the whole volume is fastened together. (A generic term, including fold sewing, oversewing, and overcasting.) To be distinguished from Stitching.

Sewing Bench—A board having two uprights connected by an adjustable bar between which and the board are stretched the tapes or cords on which the book is to be sewed. Also called Sewing Frame and Sewing Rack.

Sewing Frame—See Sewing Bench

Sewing Rack—See Sewing Bench

Sewing Through the Folds—See Fold Sewing

Shelf Back—See Backbone

Shelf Number—See Call Number

Sheets—An impression of the type as set up in the form. Sheets folded and trimmed are referred to as signatures.

Shoulder—See Ridge

Side—1. The front (or back) of a bound volume. 2. The paper, cloth or other material used on a cover face. Also called Siding.

Side Lettering—See Side Title

Side Stitching—Stitching together single leaves or sections near the binding edge, with thread or wire from front to back through the entire thickness of the leaves or sections. Distinguished from Saddle Stitching. Also called Flat Sewing and Flat Stitching.

Side Title—A title impressed on the front cover of a bound volume.

Siding—See Side

Signature—A sheet of paper consisting of two or more leaves folded and ready to be incorporated in the body of a book. Also the letter or figure placed at the bottom of the first page of each section of a book or pamphlet.

Singer Sewing—Side stitching with thread. The sewing extends the full length of the volume.

Sized Paper—Paper treated with a "starchy" material that fills the pores of the surface of the paper to prevent or retard the penetration of liquid.

Sizing—The process of applying a suitable bond between binding material and lettering.

Slide Box—See Slipcase

Slide Case—See Slipcase

Slip-in Case—See Slipcase

Slipcase—A box designed to protect a volume, covering it so that its back only is exposed. Also called Slide Case, Slip-in Case, Open-back Case, and Slide Box. See also Solander Case.

Smyth Sewing—Fold sewing done on a Smyth sewing machine. The usual kind of sewing in edition binding, commonly done without tapes, but may be done with them.

Solander—See Solander Case

Solander Box—See Solander Case

Solander Case—A book-shaped box for holding a book, pamphlets, or other material, named for its inventor, D. C. Solander. It may open on side or front with hinges, or have two separate parts, one fitting over the other. Also called Solander, Solander Box and Solander Case.

Solander Cover—See Solander Case

Special Volume—Any undersized, oversized or odd-sized volume or any volume that requires special handling.

Specification Slip—See Binding Slip

Spew—Material that exudes or is extruded. An oily or gummy exudate on the surface of a binding. Also spelled: Spue

Spine—See Backbone

Spiral Binding—A patented form of binding in which a row of fine holes is drilled through the leaves (trimmed so that each leaf is separate) and a continuous spiral-twisted wire is drawn through the holes. Also known as Coil Binding.

Sponging—The process of dampening with a wet sponge as in preparing wrinkled newspapers for pressing.

Spring Back—See Loose Back

Sprinkled Edges—Book edges on which color has been irregularly sprinkled or sprayed.

Spue—See Spew

Square—Portion of binding cover that projects beyond the signatures.

Square Corner—A book corner in which a piece of the covering material is cut out at the corner so that one turn-in of the covering material considerably overlaps the other without additional folding.

Squares—The portion of the edges of a book cover that project beyond the paper body of the book.

Stained Edges—Book edges that have been stained with color.

Stamping—Impression of tool or punch made in the outer surface of a binding.

Standard or Regular Finish—LBI library non-glossy heavy duty finish.

Standardized Lettering—A simplified method of lettering bound magazine volumes, in which all unnecessary words, abbreviations, or decorations are omitted. Years and months are placed in alignment on volumes of all sizes and titles are placed in alignment within each group size.

Standing Instructions—Instructions given binder in lieu of preparing a binding slip for each volume. A "blanket order" to your binder.

Standing Press—A vertical press in which printed and folded sheets or bound books are piled and pressed.

Staple—In pamphlet and magazine binding, one of the several clinched wire fastenings used in wire stitching.

Starch-filled—Referring to a fabric the interstices of which are filled with starch.

Stippled Edge—The edge of a volume which has been spotted irregularly with ink or dye.

Stitching—In bookbinding, the fastening together of the leaves by means of thread or wire, each single passage of the threaded needle or wire going through the bulk of the volume. (A generic term, including side stitching and saddle stitching.) To be distinguished from Sewing.

Stub—1. A narrow strip of paper, muslin or other thin material sewed in between sections, for attaching folded maps or other material of extra bulk. A cancel is usually mounted on the stub of a canceled leaf. Also known as Guard. 2. The remaining portion of a leaf cut out of a volume.

Super—See Crash

Tail—1. The bottom portion of the backbone of a bound volume. 2. The bottom portion of a page.

Tailband—See Headband

Tailcap—The covering material that has been shaped over the tailbands at the foot of the backbone of a book.

Tapes—Pieces of tape, or strips of cloth to which sections are sewed and whose free ends are pasted to the boards, or inserted between the split boards of the book covers to lend strength to the binding. Cf. Bands and Cords.

Three-quarter Binding—Binding similar to half binding, except that the leather extends further on the sides, theoretically to three-quarters of half the width of the sides. Corners are proportionately large.

Tight Back—The back of a volume in which the covering material has been glued to the back. Confined mostly to leather-backed books.

Tip In or Tipping In—To paste a leaf (or leaves) onto a printed sheet or into a bound book, without guards.

Title Leaf—See Title Page

Title Page—A page at the beginning of a book or work bearing the full title and usually also author (if any), publisher, place and date of publication, and/or other data. Sometimes called Title Leaf.

Trim—To cut the edge of a leaf or group of leaves of a volume.

Trim—1. The portion cut off in trimming. 2. The edge after trimming.

Trimmed Flush—See Cut Flush

Turn-in—The portion of a volume cover formed by turning in the cover material over the outer edges of the boards.

Two Along—In bookbinding, a method of sewing on bands, tapes or cords that treats two adjoining sections as a single unit, a method generally used for thick volumes, composed of thin sections, to avoid making the bound volume too thick at the back. Also known as Two On and Two Sheets On.

Two On—See Two Along

Two Sheets On—See Two Along

Uncut Edges—Edges of a volume that have not been trimmed in any way. Also called Untrimmed Edges. Cf. Deckle Edges.

Untrimmed Edges—See Uncut Edges

Vellum—An animal skin that has been treated with lime and stretched and scraped rather than tanned. Used for writing and printing special volumes, or for binding certain books. Sheepskin "vellum" is generally known as *Parchment*.

Verso—The left-hand page in an open book, usually bearing the even page number. Also, the back of a separate printed sheet. Formerly called Folio Verso.

Visible Joint—A cloth book joint, so made that it can be seen in the finished book.

Volume—1. Any group of leaves of a book, magazine or newspaper, bound together. 2. All the issues of a given publication issued within a specified publication period; usually the consecutive numbers of a magazine for six months or a year. 3. For library statistical purposes, any printed, typewritten, mimeographed or processed work, bound or unbound, which has been catalogued and fully prepared for use. In connection with circulation, the term volume applies to a pamphlet or a periodical as well as a book.

Warp—The threads that run the long way in fabrics.

Waterproofing—Lacquer or other waterproof material applied over lettering.

Whipstitching—See Overcasting

White-Tawed Pigskin—Pigskin converted into white leather by tanning with alum, salt, and other minerals.

Whole Binding—See Full Binding

Wire Stitch or Wire Stitching—To stitch (a pamphlet or a magazine) with wire staples, either side-fashion (side stitch) or saddle fashion (saddle stitch).

Wrapper—See Book Jacket

APPENDIX 6

HOW WE DETERMINE OUR BINDING BUDGET

By WILLIAM WEBB, *Librarian, Public Library, Flint, Michigan*

Reprinted from The Library Binder
VOLUME III, NUMBER 2, AUGUST, 1955

The Flint Public Library has for many years been more of a book circulating than a library with large reference services. The main building was constructed 50 years ago, when Flint had a population of about 15,000. In 1950 it had over 163,000 people and has had a considerable growth since that time. High school libraries have been part of the library set up. There is the Main Building (which houses adult circulation and reference only; library offices, catalog, branch, order and schools department and Main overflow is in another building 10 blocks away). A Central Children's library (3 blocks from Main) in a room in a school building; 8 branch libraries (7 in schools and 1 in a community building); a junior college, three senior and 5 junior highs. In addition there is service given to three hospitals. Collections are sent to all elementary schools in the city that do not have branch libraries; these being classroom collections in all lower grades and in upper grades of non-platooned schools and platoon collections in schools where the upper 3 grades were platooned. There are some summer stations and other small miscellaneous loaning agencies.

Budgeting for binding came through budgeting for book buying. We tried to find out, in relation to loans, how many books we had to buy each year in order to keep our collection where it was in terms of potential use and then what we had to add for growth. In the 26 years, 1928-54, Flint loaned 29,307,383 items. During that period it withdrew 329,815 volumes. Loans per withdrawal were 88.86. This included books that were worn out, became too dirty, lost and withdrawals through obsolescence. Comparing yearly figures it was found that when we did not discard or withdraw in proportion to use we had a larger number of loans per withdrawal but when we caught up on our withdrawals a number of loans per withdrawal was much lower. We had merely postponed the inevitable. The figure per withdrawal for 1928-45 was 93.1, for 1928-51 it was 88.3 and 1951-54 showed 93.5 loans per withdrawal.

Magazines are loaned in certain cases and they are included in total loans and no deductions made.

The next step was to attempt to relate binding to loans. We have no statistics on how many of our discards were bound and how many unbound. Such would help our figures. On the other hand this would be difficult to get unless we had time to evaluate the book at the time we discarded it. So we come to the proposition of some average over-all figures. We know that a book, to have a long life, must be rebound. We also know that some books are used for part of their life, but never enough to be rebound. Some rebinds are discarded before the life of the rebinding is used up. This means that we cannot say that every 88.86 loans means a rebinding. If we divide 88.86 into our loans we would need to have rebound 12,400 books in 1953-54. Actually we rebound about 8,600 or one for each 129 loans. Other years approximate those figures. We use 125 loans as meaning we must have a rebind.

Prebinding

This has not been included in binding costs, but is in the book budget. Many easy books and primers are bought prebound and the price is a unit and it would be difficult to separate and charge to binding. Other books bought prebound are mainly large ones and some in board covers.

We do not do much prebinding of ordinary sized volumes. Regular rebinding may cost a bit more and may take some extra handling, but much of this handling can be done by students and is not too costly for labor. Getting two new covers during the life of a book is worth the extra cost. We expect to get some extra circulations to repay our extra outlay. In addition should the book be lost or damaged before rebinding we have a smaller investment that is lost.

Books in publishers' covers have 15 to 40 loans before rebinding; 25 loans is a very good average. At that rate a book costing us $2.00 costs 8 cents per loan. If rebinding costs $1.20 it takes 15 loans at the same rate to pay out our binding investment. Any loans beyond that starts cutting our cost per loan. If this book that is rebound circulates 100 times our average cost per loan is 3.2 cents. The same book prebound may become inattractive or too dirty and we may get only 85 or 90 loans in all and in such cases our cost per loan is 3.76 or 3.55 cents. In this connection there is another cost in that we must reorder sooner and reordering and processing of new books takes much more time than handling for rebinding.

So our calculation of 125 loans meaning one rebinding presumes the buying of some easies and primers and large books in prebound condition. And these charges are not in our binding budget.

Kinds and Age of Collections

Our figures are based on an established and going collection. A new collection can easily call for a lower loan figure than a 125. We don't have enough experience with new agencies to do more than hazard a guess.

A new branch with 10,000 new books might loan 75,000 volumes a year or 7.5 loans per volume. If no new books were added to take up part of the use, the possible loans before binding would be 25 x 10,000 or 250,000, or three and one third years of use. On this basis we cannot use the 125 figure of loans per rebinding, as it would give us 2,000 rebinds. On the other hand we will rebind some books at the end of a year and more during the second year and loans of these rebound books will take up some of the use. New books will also take up more of the use. However we should expect to bind more than the 2,000 volumes over 125 figure provides for. Taking all allowances into consideration there should be an extra binding allowance for new collections for the second through the fifth year. A guess is 150 loans per binding the first year, 75 the second year, 50 the third year through the fifth.

Other Influences

This theory of calculating rebinding costs likely may vary from library to library. Individual ideas as to how fresh looking a book should be to be kept may affect the figure. How good is the care of books by borrowers can affect it. We know in some branches books get dirtier quicker and get harder wear. Also affecting it is whether you are increasing the size of the collection by buying more books than needed to keep the collection going with the same potential use (i.e. if we buy more than 1 book for each 88.86 loans). These extra new books can temporarily take up part of the 125 loans. However eventually many of them will need binding.

Calculating Costs

So far we have talked only of calculating rebinds in terms of loans. How do you determine the actual amount of money needed?

1. Magazines are calculated separately. Get the number and size of volumes rebound each year and multiply by costs.

2. Reference Books in the Flint set up are not a great volume and we ignore as a separate item. Others may have to figure separately.

3. We did not like the system of charging by size, extra charges by call numbers, etc. It means extra time in bindery and extra time for us to check bills and charge (we keep separate accounts of amount spent for each agency).

4. Some years ago we took all our bills over a 2-year period for all books other than magazines under the "by size" system. We totalled those of each size and how many call numbers, etc. We got the average cost per book. We then asked for unit prices on our rebinding. A unit system saves binderies something in measuring, counting, extras, etc. We guarantee a certain volume of work. Flint's volume may differ from other libraries. Also the make up of the work may vary as to number of large books, call numbers, etc. But most libraries can likely find out from their binding records what proportion of various sizes are bound, how many call numbers and symbols and extras there are should be able to find their own average costs.

5. We estimate our loans, divide by 125, and multiplied by our unit cost. Then we add our magazine binding and make allowances for any extras for books bought beyond replacement needs and any new agencies and add all of these in.

Conclusion

This system of calculating book funds and binding is one that a business man can understand.

We also make the point that rebinding is a service charge to get the full value out of a book. This system of calculating binding budgets must be tailored to meet individual conditions. It will likely not apply to colleges and universities. They have large reserve book collections. It may not be applicable to all public libraries. It is definitely based in part on guesswork and rule of thumb but does work well.

There are a lot of questions that if answered could give us a better picture. How about juvenile and adult books? In 1951 we stopped counting these separately. In the period 1928-1951 our figures had an average of 88.3 loans per withdrawal for all books, while adult was 84.3 and juvenile 91.3. Tentative figures show "easies" had lower figures than the average.

APPENDIX 7

SIGNIFICANT DATA—GROWTH
1957-1968

	1957, 58 or 59	1968	% Increase
1. U.S. Population	170,510,000[1]	204,146,000[2]	19.7%
2. Libraries in U.S.	12,852[3]	27,746[4]	116%
3. Books, Periodicals & Binding	$132,412,000[5]	$455,707,000[5]	244.9%
4. Books	$ 95,285,000[5]	$347,965,000[5]	265.9%
5. Periodicals	$ 24,449,000[5]	$ 65,264,000[5]	170.0%
6. Binding	$ 13,825,000[5]	$ 31,371,000[5]	127.0%
7. LBI Members' Sales	$ 8,027,000[6]	$ 27,117,000[6]	237.0%
8. Price: Rebind 8″ Book	$ 1.81[7]	$ 2.50[8]	38.1%
9. Price: Rebind 12″ Perio	$ 3.68[7]	$ 4.75[8]	29.0%
10. Price: Selected Hardcover Books	$ 5.29[9]	$ 8.47[9]	60.1%
11. Price: Periodicals	$ 4.92[9]	$ 8.65[9]	75.8%
12. Price: Serial Service	$39.80[9]	$70.87[9]	78.1%

[1] Bowker Annual '59 p. 3 (1957).
[2] Bowker Annual '69 p. 3 (1968).
[3] Bowker Annual '59 p. 5 (1957).
[4] Bowker Annual '69 p. 7 (1968).
[5] Bowker Annual '69 pp. 5, 6.
[6] LBI Meeting Reports (1959 & 1968 Sales).
[7] LBI Survey 1958.
[8] LBI Survey 1968
[9] Bowker Annual '69 pp. 47, 48, 49.

SURVEYS ON THE MAINTENANCE
OF LIBRARY MATERIALS

Reprinted from The Library Binder, *Volume XVII—No. 2, December, 1969*

The availability of usable library statistics is limited, as was pointed out by the Report of the National Advisory Commission on Libraries.

But the need for certain types of data is a continuing one and since 1965 the Library Binding Institute has periodically conducted surveys intended to furnish some basic and rather elementary data about the use of library binding to conserve or maintain library collections. The first survey was made in 1954 under the auspices of the American Library Association—Library Binding Institute Joint Committee, using a representative sample furnished by the Americai Library Association. This survey was repeated in substantially the same form in 1960. The third survey, in 1964, used as a sample a list furnished by the R. R. Bowker Company. The most comprehensive survey was conducted in 1968,* using Bowker lists, and forms were sent to Public Libraries, College and University Libraries, Junior College Libraries, County and Regional Libraries and Business and Technical Libraries.

Based on these surveys, some interesting observations can be made, covering most of the past two decades:

1. In 1954 and in 1968 about 90% of American libraries specified "Class A" (now LBI Standard) for 75%-100% of their rebinding of worn volumes and initial hardcover binding of periodicals.

2. One of the reasons for this lies in the strength of "Class A" binding. In the earlier surveys, the returns indicated many libraries kept circulation records. The 1968 returns indicated few kept any such records. What records, tests and other studies there are indicate about a 4-1 ratio of the wearability of "Class A" volumes to trade volumes, including publishers' reinforced bindings. Similarly, the comments by librarians consistently refer to the inadequacy of publishers' editions for library use. By contrast, a librarian may reasonably expect about 100 circulations or uses from a "Class A" bound volume.

The reason for the strength of "Class A" bound volumes is that the LBI Standard specifies the materials and methods to be used. This is in contrast to publishers' editions where there are no uniform specifications other than for textbooks.

3. Equally significant is the conclusion that the absence of specific requirements for materials and methods when coupled with a lack of record keeping of circulations, renders meaningless the various "guarantees" of numbers of circulations or any standard not geared to construction specifications which are definite and which have been proven by experience to meet library requirements. It would appear that a library is best protected by specifying LBI Standard binding and requiring the Warranty that all Certified Library Binders are required to affix to their invoices.

4. In the two most recent surveys, a question was asked about what it cost to put a volume on the shelf, ready for reader use, excluding the cost of the volume. The amazing part of the answers is the fact that so few libraries know what such costs are. It would seem that this cost would be so fundamental to the operation of a library that it would be constantly kept and reviewed.

In this connection, what also is surprising is the tremendous range in estimates as to this cost.

5. Library binding as an expenditure is usually placed in a general overhead or expense classification and not usually carried as a separate account classification such as is the case in the acquisition of books. By and large, all library classifications, except public libraries, increased the expenditures for library binding as a per cent of total budget be-

tween 1967-1968. This is encouraging, since during this period libraries have been involved in major programs of acquisition, and budgeting for the maintenance of a book or periodical should be done at or near the time of acquisition.

6. In these days of high prices and inflation, it is a credit to the library binding industry that its prices have increased at a rate substantially less than that of new books, periodicals or serials. Between 1957 and 1968, the price of selected hardcover books increased about 60%, whereas the price of rebinding an 8" volume increased only about 38%. Periodicals and serial services increased about 75% during this period but the price of binding a 12" periodical increased only 29% during this period.

This good record has been accomplished in the face of increases in labor costs, with the average hourly cost rising approximately 75%, and in all other expenses of library binders and is the result of new equipment and sound management practices. LBI members' sales increased about 237% during this period. The following chart, which is not part of the survey, highlights some significant data.

Summary of 1968 Survey
On Maintenance of Library Materials

QUESTION #1: *Of your books and periodicals that are rebound, approximately what percentage is done according to the LBI Standard for Library Binding (based upon the Minimum Specifications for Class A Library Binding of ALA and LBI)?*

(Check one)——100%   ——75-100%
          ——50-75%   ——25-50%
          ——Under 25%

This question is designed to elicit information as to the use of the LBI Standard by libraries. The answers indicated that by and large the pattern of the last several years prevails—most American libraries specify LBI Standard (Class A) for most of their rebinding.

71% of the replies indicated that they used LBI Standard for 100% of their rebinding.
88% indicated they used the Standard for 75%-100% of their work.

The respective percentages of different kinds of libraries is as follows, for 75%-100% of their work:

Colleges and Universities	85%
Junior Colleges	95%
Public Libraries	88%
County and Regional	89%
Business & Technical	82%

QUESTION #2: *What is the* approximate *average circulation of books bound in* LIBRARY *binding?*

QUESTION #3: *What is the* approximate *average circulation of books bound in publishers' binding?*

The answers to these questions represented the greatest change since 1964 survey. The average number of circulations of Class "A" volumes in academic and public libraries was about 91. About half of the public libraries reported over 100 circulations. Publishers' editions averaged 27.5 circulations. Almost 50% of these answers ranged from 15-25 circulations. Less than 5% of the libraries who answered these questions in 1966 kept records of circulations and only about one-third of the total who replied answered this question.

Thus, of about 800 replies, only 9 answered that they had actual figures of circulation for library binding and 14 for publishers' bindings.

The most reliable current data on circulations is that obtained by the Library Technology Project. The Fourth Annual Report stated that:

". . . the laboratory (W. J. Barrow Research Laboratory in Richmond, Virginia) had tested 260 "Class A" bound books and 240 books in publishers' bindings, out of a total of 800 copies of each type. These books were specifically purchased and half of them rebound in "Class A" binding to provide samples for an evaluation of the Universal Tester. Preliminary results of the tests performed on trade bindings and upon the same books bound according to "Class A" bindings showed even greater durability, with no observable damage after four times the average number of revolutions required to produce moderate damage in publishers' bindings."

QUESTION #4: *Do you know the approximate cost of putting a volume on the shelf, ready for reader use,* EXCLUDING *the cost of the volume?*

The answers to this were quite startling, since they reveal that by and large libraries do not know what it costs to put a book on the shelf. The following table sums up the answers:

Kinds of Library	*% That Know Cost*	*Average Cost*	*Range*
College & University	39%	$4.51	52c-$15.00
College & University (over 500,000 volumes)	40%	4.94	52c-$13.00
Junior College	44%	3.20	35c-$12.00
Public Libraries	51%	2.68	30c-$20.00
Public Libraries (over 500,000 volumes)	52%	3.61	1.16-$20.00
County & Regional	45%	1.65	55c-$ 3.85
County & Regional (over 500,000 volumes)	58%	1.75	1.13-$ 2.40
Business & Technical	24%	5.25	75c-$10.00

QUESTION #5: *What is the most recent* average *price paid by you for library binding?*

The following two tables show prices paid for different sizes of books and periodicals.

BOOK BINDING

	8"	9"	10"	12"	Average
COLLEGE & UNIV. LIBRARIES	$1.96	$2.09	$2.56	$3.09	$2.55
Range	$ .94-$5.00	$ .94-$ 5.25	$1.30-$ 6.75	$1.30-$ 6.85	$1.00-$ 6.00
JUNIOR COLLEGE LIBRARIES	$1.84	$2.17	$2.55	$2.95	$2.41
Range	$1.25-$3.90	$1.25-$ 3.75	$1.90-$ 4.25	$1.25-$ 4.25	$1.25-$ 7.00
PUBLIC LIBRARIES	$1.85	$2.14	$2.39	$2.86	$2.34
Range	$1.10-$3.90	$1.13-$ 3.90	$1.13-$ 3.95	$1.13-$ 5.34	$1.13-$ 4.45
COUNTY & REGIONAL LIBRARIES	$1.83	$2.11	$2.43	$2.85	$2.19
Range	$1.25-$3.00	$1.39-$ 3.50	$1.70-$ 3.95	$1.80-$ 4.40	$1.15-$ 3.75
BUSINESS & TECHNICAL LIBRARIES	$3.08	$3.27	$3.58	$3.67	$3.99
Range	$1.65-$ 9.00	$1.80-$10.00	$1.80-$12.00	$1.80-$ 5.50	$1.80-$10.50

PERIODICAL BINDING

	10"	12"	14"	16"	Average
COLLEGE & UNIV. LIBRARIES	$4.13	$4.63	$5.22	$5.78	$4.71
Range	$1.60-$12.00	$1.90-$12.25	$2.05-$12.50	$2.15-$12.75	$1.94-$12.38
JUNIOR COLLEGE LIBRARIES	$4.12	$4.65	$5.27	$5.75	$4.85
Range	$2.25-$ 4.90	$2.75-$ 5.50	$3.30-$ 6.10	$3.75-$ 7.05	$3.03-$ 7.90
PUBLIC LIBRARIES	$4.28	$4.79	$5.43	$5.87	$4.75
Range	$1.00-$ 7.50	$2.75-$ 8.00	$2.75-$ 8.38	$2.75-$ 8.50	$2.71-$ 7.83
COUNTY & REGIONAL LIBRARIES	$4.26	$4.93	$5.37	$5.91	$4.73
Range	$2.70-$ 9.87	$3.20-$ 8.00	$3.55-$ 8.00	$3.75-$ 7.50	$2.75-$ 7.15
BUSINESS & TECHNICAL LIBRARIES	$4.73	$5.18	$5.55	$5.97	$5.16
Range	$3.00-$14.25	$3.00-$ 8.10	$3.50-$ 8.10	$3.50-$ 7.95	$3.00-$14.25

QUESTION #6: *What per cent of your total budget was allocated to library binding?*

Public libraries' answers showed a small decline in the percentage of budget allocated to library binding in 1968 compared with 1967. The average in 1967 was 4.68% compared with 4.45% in 1968. These do not correlate with Bowker figures which indicate a larger drop, but these are the averages of about 100 of the libraries who answered this question.

All others showed increases as follows:

Library	1967	1968
College & University	7.84%	9.35%
Junior College	4.34%	5.4%
Regional	2.9%	3.4%
Business & Technical	6.5%	7.0%

QUESTION #7: *What is the one single thing which (in your opinion) would improve a librarian's task of maintaining collections?*

COMMENTS MOST OFTEN MADE WERE:

"Better publishers' bindings" (This was noted by a large majority of those who commented.)
"Wider inner margins so books could be rebound"
"More money for binding"
"Faster service by binderies"

SOME COMMENTS OF PARTICULAR INTEREST:

"Perhaps the biggest improvement in binding of periodicals would be the expansion of the plan where binders receive copies of subscriptions for heavily used titles and send the bound volumes to the library, eliminating the need to take these titles out of use or maintain records for locally received binding copy subscriptions."
"If all publishers could be required, by law, to use oversewn bindings in their hardback books."
"Instruction in library school on how to recognize whether a book or pamphlet needs binding, mending, recasing, slipcase, pamphlet binding, etc., and an obligatory visit to a bindery."
"Another thing that would help would be for LBI to sponsor a good standard method of perfect binding that all LBI members would offer in addition to Class A so that some distinction could be made between materials that will receive heavy use and those that will not."
"Reduction in overhead of preparing binding instructions through use of standard systems that would be closely compatible with systems and patterns used earlier by the libraries."
"Standardization of binding data—Color, lettering position and style, etc."
"May I cast my vote against the trend of larger and larger books— they will not fit on library shelves, they are too heavy to hold, and the binding will probably prove to be inadequate."
"Publish all books sold to library collections in library binding and better quality paper so it wouldn't yellow."

"Uniformity of journal size wherever possible—changing size in middle of volume should be definitely avoided."

"To get LC cards with the books." (A number of people said this.)

"Library binding of all highly recommended books for school collections."

"Stop postponing binding decisions for forty years, and temporizing with homemade repairs until the entire book collection takes on an appearance so repulsive that no browser wants to reach out and take a volume off the shelf. Eventually, somebody has to come along and clean up the mess."

"Somebody, perhaps LBI, or the library schools, must make librarians aware that collection maintenance is a task that must be approached on a continuous and systematic basis and not postponed. Also, the people who are making the binding decisions ought to be made aware of the fact that they are not saving any by attempting major repairs with home-made methods."

"Publishers could cooperate to a greater extent by not putting important material on endpapers, but they have not cooperated in this respect, despite repeated requests over the years. It doesn't seem likely they will cooperate in the future."

"I suggest an LBI film, to be shown at national and state meetings, setting forth the facts of life."

"We would like wider margins on trade bindings which must invariably be rebound. We object to so-called library bindings (publishers) which do not equal rebindings' durability. We feel we are being cheated when we see we pay net price for a book only to have it arrive in a publishers' library binding that is too tightly sewn and that does not last as long as a standard rebinding job."

"I think we already have that with us—good binding according to accepted code. Nothing else (outside of microfilm) can maintain the book stock for hard public use."

"An adequate appropriation for the binding and rebinding of books."

"Uniformity and improvement of quality in publishers' bindings including their so-called 'library bindings.'

Their use now of the plastic glue rather than sewing is a poor substitute, also hinges are quite often nothing but paper. These are two causes of much of our trouble. There is no uniformity in 'publishers' library binding'. Many are poorly sewn and the cloth used tears easily."

"Although better binding and better paper would help, wider adoption by publishers of formats that lend themselves to binding, i.e., wider inside margins, etc., would help most."

"The use of acid-free or low acid 'permanent' paper by the original publishers. Many times a book must be replaced since rebinding is not advisable because the inner pages of the book are yellowed and brittle.

Where this is not possible—a process used by which an alkali treatment could be given the pages at a reasonable cost, to reduce effect of atmospheric conditions on the acids in the paper."

"Cooperation with higher management in recognizing the need to raise and maintain *high* standards of binding; admission that nothing —including cheap binding—is a bargain if it can't be used. Sub-standard binding is shoddy and sometimes defaces the valuable publications we try to keep."

"Outside of *additional* and sufficient *funds* in the budget for binding, the most important thing needed to improve the maintenance of the book collection is the *staff time* to systematically examine the book collection, pull off materials for rebinding, and prepare them for the bindery—records, lists, etc."

"Stronger cloth and adhesive in hinges when contents are fastened to the covers by publishers."

"Library bindings for all volumes added to general library collections."

"With respect to binding, a four week turn-around time for materials requiring binding would be immensely helpful."

"The allocation of sufficient funds to hire a full-time civil service person (library technician) whose sole responsibility would be to be in charge of the maintenance of all materials throughout the library.

Prebound paperbacks and serials which a college library could get (in sufficient number of duplicate copies of same title) and all ready to put on the shelf. A consultant service to help the librarian go over his messy collection so he could know where to start and perhaps have some idea of how much it would cost to preserve the mouldering 'core' of it."

"A comprehensive set of standards which would accurately identify materials in need of rebinding early and a reduced rebinding time period which would permit the early return of materials for circulation."

"Reduction in overhead of preparing binding instructions through use of standard systems that would be closely compatible with systems and patterns used earlier by the libraries. This could be based on an alpha-numerical method of designating size and style of type, and a numerical designation for height of lettering above the shelf. This latter would be based on statistical analysis of library holdings. My own studies show some 30 different heights seem to match 90% of the variations. Preprinted binding slips for common titles, allowing the library to designate height and lettering would be a savings to many. Present mechanized systems vary too much from one contract to another. As we are required to get bids frequently, we cannot have sure continuity of binders.

Part of this problem could be solved by having LBI members instructed in the meanings of various ways of writing call numbers, importance of position and punctuation of the numbers, and other library usages. Most binders, and few retail booksellers neither know nor care about the problems of description and uniform entry and uniform nomenclature in libraries. Therefore, added research in buying books, added notation and explanation to binders on how to write call numbers, etc., is needed. Then . . . the boy at the lettering machine goofs it up anyhow.

Instruction in balance and good taste would be useful to many of the people now either using or designing lettering equipment. Original type-writer machines for spine lettering used an illegible type font. Present people either get heavy handed and use 72 point type on little books or 10 point in the middle of a vast spine. Judgment seems rare.

The above are my own views, and are suggestions rather than doctrine of the library. My views are based on experience as Chief of Acquisitions and some 30 years of librarianship, of which 6½ involved supervision of a fully equipped library owned bindery."

"All books be bound according to LBI Standard for Class A. library bindings of ALA and LBI."

"A more adequate budget. A better way to control loss of books by theft." (Note: This was the first survey in which theft and abuse by patrons was as frequently mentioned.)

"Being a public institution, we must let bids on a competitive basis each year for services such as binding. We have been fortunate in that the bid usually goes to a bindery who is a member of LBI each year. But, our experience one year with a binder who was not a member of LBI (but who had agreed to do work meeting LBI standards) causes us to wish that membership in LBI could be used as a factor in bid specifications. The promptness, courtesy, and other intangible qualities of the LBI bindery far outweighed the few cents' difference between its prices and the non-LBI bindery's prices that year."

"If the publishers of periodicals would have their volumes correspond with calendar year. Some still start in September and end in June. If art book publishers would discontinue publication of books over 12 inches."

"If books were well bound in the first place it would help a great deal. We have to return more and more books to the jobber that are coming out of the backs when we get them. Some are bound in upside down, or assembled incorrectly. If they have been inadvertently processed, we may have to mend them before they are ever loaned."

"Standardization of binding data—color, lettering position and style, etc."

"Continuous education of staff members responsible for shelving books and withdrawing books for mending or rebinding from returned books at circulation desk.

"Purchase larger quantity of pre-bound books—would prefer good trade edition that could be rebound in first quality buckram to publishers' library edition.

"Improved methods of gluing (perhaps better glue) for trade editions."

"A systematic and continuous review of the collection (by classification categories) that would afford an evaluation of the total collection at least every other year. Newly published acquisitions would continue to be added to the collection as usual, but this continuous review procedure would:

1. Provide a retrospective analysis of a particular classification.
2. Constitute the basis for replacement orders as necessary.
3. Schedule weeding on a planned basis.
4. Pull books for binding and/or mending.

Too many libraries concentrate entirely or almost entirely on new book selection and acquisition with no real procedure for a regular retrospective analysis of the collection. Unless the latter is scheduled, it is rarely accomplished."

"Uniformity of journal size wherever possible—changing size in middle of volume should definitely be avoided."

"Uniformity by all publishers in format: Preferably title page and table of contents in front and index in last issue, at back and not in the middle of last issue. If title page must be included in last issue, author index should not be started on the back of the T.P. Some libraries much prefer T.P. in front and index in back of volume.

When one volume has to be bound in 2 or more sections, title page should be in first issue for each section.

"Volume, issue numbers and date should be in a prominent place on cover and spine. This would save considerable time in logging in journals as well as in binding preparation."

"Name changes in journal title—great confusion caused when this occurs in mid-year, i.e., *Printer's Ink* changed to *Marketing/Communications* in October. It would also help if the journal changing its name would begin new title with Vol. 1.

Example: J. *Gas Chromatography,* Vols. 1-6 changed name to J. *Chromatographic Science,* beginning with Vol. 7.

When shelving alphabetically by journal title, this leads to complications and cross references."

"Journals should avoid publishing issues of split years, such as Dec.-Jan. 1967-68. This particular journal could just as easily have published the issue to cover Nov.-Dec."

"I think that all binderies should have a standard color and a standard spine identification (including LC number) for each specific periodical. Further, I think it would be to the advantage of the binderies to publish a yearly handbook of recommended standards for binding colors for periodicals, recommended standards for spine imprinting and recommended size (number of issues) per volume."

"I think that all publications, books and periodicals that are bound should contain a shelf identification number (LC or Dewey). This should not only apply to rebinding but to new publications. A standard place, standard size for all publications."

"Services to locate missing copies and magazines."

"Convert to microfilm cartridge."

"Our main concern at the present time is that journals are bound so close to the printing that xeroxing copies is next to impossible in some cases. We have spoken to our binder about this and he feels that this can only be improved with the cooperation of the printer. Could the Institute be effective in bringing about such cooperation?"

"Some conformity in publishing and publishers' procedures such as:

No repetition of volume numbers.
Consistent size issues throughout year.
Definite annual or volume indexes—preferably appearing in the last issue.
Maintain same title throughout volume or year."

"One thing that I think all librarians would like to see is a better original binding on periodicals. Many times the binding is broken before the book or periodical (paper bound) is ever sent for binding. We have a very small circulation and experience this, so the problem must be much greater in some libraries."

"Publishers must give wider inner margins so that we can photocopy pages after a volume is bound."

"Enough clerical help and efficient cataloging."

"If binding delivery could be cut down to three weeks."

"More uniformity in the formats of journals would help considerably. Journals should be given volume numbers which change when a sufficient number of pages have appeared to make a manageable volume. Journal publishers should avoid the long volume which must be bound in parts and these have an index for one part bound in another part."

"Publishers should have large inner margins particularly in large volumes to allow for good reproduction when making photocopies. Publishers should allow for trimming when they lay out their work, so that information will not be lost. Folded illustrations should be folded to allow for trimming."

"Binders should adopt new washable (plastic) binding materials and give up old-fashioned cloth covers which are ruined when they get wet or dirty."

"Prompt return of volumes from bindery."

"Some method to speed cataloging by subject."

"The one practice in the binding of periodicals and maintenance of map collections which would improve the librarian's task of maintaining collections is the standardization of format and size and also spine lettering."

"Space is our greatest problem. We are turning to microfilm for materials older than five years, except in the case of society journals, which we bind."

"Many so-called publishers' bindings are inferior and come apart in a short time. But librarians, special librarians especially, have little choice but to buy, whatever the binding."

APPENDIX 8

LIBRARY BINDING INSTITUTE
160 State Street—Boston, Massachusetts 02109

QUALITY CONTROL INSPECTION REPORT

This form is the Quality Control Inspection Report used by the Co-ordinator in connection with the Quality Control Program of the Library Binding Institute.

Every Certified Library Binder, prior to certification, is inspected in order to determine his capability of binding volumes which conform to the Library Binding Institute Standard for library binding. After certification, every binder is periodically inspected. A copy of the report is given to the responsible officer of the Certified Library Bindery and a copy is sent to the Executive Director of Library Binding Institute whose responsibility it is to follow up on any deviations from the Standard.

Volumes bound according to the Library Binding Institute Standard may be expected to withstand one hundred or more circulations or uses under normal library conditions. In addition, the volumes are completely collated for reader usability. Conformity to the specifications requires both the use of specified materials and careful workmanship. The purpose of the In-Plant Quality Control Program is the assurance that libraries who are the principal customers of Certified Library Binders receive qualified library binding, thereby assuring the lowest cost per circulation or use.

Every Certified Library Binder is required to affix a warranty to his invoices stating that the binding covered by the invoice meets the Library Binding Institute Standard unless specifically noted otherwise.

QUALITY CONTROL INSPECTION REPORT

BINDERY _____ADDRESS _____

Person   Date of
Interviewed _____Inspection _____

	Complies With Specification	
	YES	NO

1.0 COLLATION AND MENDING
1.1 Handled properly ____ ____
1.2 Mending complete ____ ____
1.3 Material used for mending: _____ ____ ____
1.4 Quality Control ____ ____

2.0 PREPARATION FOR SEWING
2.1 Maps and inserts set out ____ ____
2.2 All possible back margin preserved by— ____ ____
       Sanding_____Paper cutter_____
       Grinding_____ ____ ____
2.3 Sections of proper thickness ____ ____
       Method used: Pad counter_____
       Machine_____Loose pages_____
2.4 Volumes with stiff paper scored ____ ____
2.5 Quality Control ____ ____

3.0 END PAPERS
3.1 Properly constructed ____ ____
       Type used_____X_____Y_____
       Z_____Other
3.2 Reinforcing fabric neatly pasted down ____ ____
3.3 Paper and reinforcing fabric correct quality ____ ____
3.4 Quality Control ____ ____

4.0 SEWING
    A. *Oversewing*
4.1   Sections proper thickness ____ ____
4.2   Sections properly pasted (if by machine) ____ ____
4.3   Proper distance from top and bottom ____ ____
4.4   Thread proper weight and quality ____ ____
           Brand:_____
4.5   Quality Control ____ ____
    B. *Side-sewing*
4.6   Thickness ½ inch or less ____ ____
4.7   Stiff paper volumes scored ____ ____
4.8   Stitches properly spaced and distanced ____ ____
           Sewing by:_____Hand_____
           Machine
4.9   Thread extensions for paste-down ____ ____
4.10   Quality Control ____ ____
    C. *Through-the-fold:*
4.11   Hand sewing on tape or cords when mar-
           gins or other conditions will not per-
           mit Oversewing ____ ____

	Complies With Specification	
	YES	NO

4.12 Signatures reinforced where necessary   _____ _____
4.13 Tapes used on books or magazines:
4.14   Height under 9 in.—2 tapes or cords   _____ _____
4.15   Height from 9 in. to 12¾ in.—3 tapes
         or cords   _____ _____
4.16   Height over 12¾ in.—4 tapes or cords   _____ _____
4.17 Newspapers and special outsize volumes—5
        or more tapes or cords depending on size   _____ _____
4.18 Thread used in all hand sewing _____   _____ _____
4.19 Quality Control   _____ _____

5.0 *FOLDING AND TIPPING*
5.1 Endsheet folds neat and even with binding
        edge   _____ _____
            Method used_____
5.2 Proper adhesion after gluing   _____ _____
5.3 Quality Control   _____ _____

6.0 *TRIMMING*
6.1 Pages trimmed square   _____ _____
6.2 Edges smooth (allowance for narrow mar-
        gins)   _____ _____
6.3 Trim size record or sample followed (peri-
        odicals)   _____ _____
6.4 Edges: Sprinkled_____Stained_____
        Plain_____   _____ _____
6.5 Quality Control   _____ _____

7.0 *GLUING*
7.1 Brand of flexible adhesive_____   _____ _____
7.2 Properly applied   _____ _____
7.3 Quality Control   _____ _____

8.0 *ROUNDING AND BACKING*
8.1 Well rounded   _____ _____
8.2 Properly backed: Method used _____   _____ _____
8.3 Quality Control   _____ _____

9.0 *BACK LINING*
9.1 Material used (volumes ½ inch or over)
        _____   _____ _____
9.2 Material used (volumes less than ½ inch)
        _____   _____ _____
9.3 Properly extends onto sides and to head and
        tail   _____ _____
9.4 Properly and firmly glued   _____ _____
9.5 Extra paper on heavy volumes   _____ _____
           Method used _____
9.6 Quality Control   _____ _____

	Complies With Specification
	YES NO

10.0 *COVERS*
10.1 Cover material meets specifications
Cloth brand—Books_____Periodicals_____   ____ ____
Board brand_____Thickness used_____
Inlay brand_____Thickness used_____
10.2 Glue evenly applied to cloth   ____ ____
10.3 Cover material evenly turned in (⅝ inch)   ____ ____
10.4 Corners neat and workmanlike   ____ ____
10.5 Joints uniform and sufficient   ____ ____
10.6 Quality Control   ____ ____

11.0 *LETTERING*
Books
11.1 Legible   ____ ____
11.2 Neatly arranged and properly centered   ____ ____
11.3 Uniformly impressed   ____ ____
11.4 23K genuine gold or better Brand_____   ____ ____
11.5 Record or rub file for sets   ____ ____
Periodicals
11.6 Legible   ____ ____
11.7 Neatly arranged and properly centered   ____ ____
11.8 Uniformly impressed   ____ ____
11.9 23K genuine gold or better Brand_____   ____ ____
11.10 Record or rub file for sets   ____ ____
11.11 Quality Control   ____ ____

12.0 *CASING-IN*
12.1 Method used___ _____
12.2 Adhesive used_____
12.3 Book properly centered in case   ____ ____
12.4 End papers firmly adhered to cover   ____ ____
12.5 Board squares uniform and proper   ____ ____
12.6 Quality Control   ____ ____

13.0 *INSPECTION*
13.1 Opened out   ____ ____
13.2 Checked for binding defects   ____ ____
13.3 Checked for lettering errors   ____ ____
13.4 Checked for cleanliness   ____ ____
13.5 Overall workmanship and general appear-
ance of volumes
Good_____Fair_____Poor_____

14.0 *WARRANTY*—Uses warranty stamp properly on all invoices:
Yes_____No_____

15.0 *COMMENTS* (Use additional sheets for comments if necessary.)

A. The Certified Library Binder is producing work in accordance with the LBI Standard and meeting the requirements of Certification.
Yes_____No_____

B. A substantial proportion of the work produced by the Certified Binder is *NOT* in accordance with the LBI Standard in workmanship or materials or both. (Explain) _____

_____

_____

C. NONE of the work in the plant conforms to LBI Standard Binding _____

_____

_____

Does plant have an adequate Quality Control Program?_____

_____

_____

DATE _____ INSPECTED BY: _____

APPENDIX 9

FEDERAL TRADE COMMISSION
Washington

TRADE PRACTICE RULES
FOR THE
LIBRARY BINDING INDUSTRY

As Promulgated August 20, 1954

STATEMENT BY THE COMMISSION:

Trade practice rules for the Library Binding Industry, as hereinafter set forth, are promulgated by the Federal Trade Commission under the trade practice conference procedure.

The rules are directed to the maintenance of free and fair competition in the industry and to the elimination and prevention of unfair methods of competition, unfair or deceptive acts or practices, and other trade abuses. To this end they afford helpful guidance to all members of the industry.

The industry for which such trade practice rules are established is composed of persons, firms, corporations, and organizations engaged in the business of rebinding and prebinding of books, periodicals, and other documents especially for use in public and private libraries.

Proceedings leading to the establishment of rules were instituted upon application by the industry. A general industry conference was held under Commission auspices in New York City at which proposals for rules were submitted for consideration of the Commission. Thereafter, a draft of proposed rules was released by the Commission and public hearing thereon was held in Washington, D. C., at which all interested or affected parties were afforded opportunity to present their views, suggestions, or objections regarding the rules.

Following such hearing, and upon consideration of the entire matter, final action was taken by the Commission whereby it approved the Group I rules hereinafter set forth. No Group II rules have been included for the reason that the Group II rules recommended by the industry are of a type presently the subject of a general study by the Commission. If, after completion of such study, it is determined that provisions of this type may be included as Group II rules for industries, an opportunity will then be afforded to the members of this industry to have such rules included.

Such rules become operative thirty (30) days from the date of promulgation.

THE RULES

These rules promulgated by the Commission are designed to foster and promote the maintenance of fair competitive conditions in the interest of protecting industry, trade, and the public. It is to this end, and to the exclusion of any act or practice which fixes or controls prices through combination or agreement, or which unreasonably restrains trade or suppresses competition, or otherwise unlawfully injures, destroys, or prevents competition, that the rules are to be applied.

INDUSTRY DEFINITION

Members of this industry are those persons, firms, corporations, and organizations engaged in the business of rebinding and prebinding of books, periodicals, and other documents especially for use in public and private libraries.

GROUP I

The unfair trade practices embraced in the Group I rules herein are considered to be unfair methods of competition, unfair or deceptive acts or practices, or other illegal practices, prohibited under laws administered by the Federal Trade Commission; and appropriate proceedings in the public interest will be taken by the Commission to prevent the use, by any person, partnership, corporation, or other organization subject to its jurisdiction, of such unlawful practices in commerce.

RULE 1—DECEPTION (GENERAL).

It is an unfair trade practice for any industry member to use, or cause or promote the use of, any advertising matter, guarantee, warranty, trade promotional literature, mark, brand, label, or other representation, however disseminated or published, which has the capacity and tendency or effect of misleading or deceiving purchasers, prospective purchasers, or the consuming public with respect to the grade, quality, conformity to a trade standard, material, composition, construction, fabrication, manufacture, distribution, origin, or price or terms of sale, of library binding, or which is false, misleading, or deceptive in any other material respect.

Among the various deceptive practices inhibited by the paragraph above are the following:

(a) *Misrepresentation as to Character of Business.* It is an unfair trade practice for any member of the industry to represent, directly or indirectly, through the use of any word or term in his corporate or trade name, in his advertising or otherwise, that he is a library binder, or that he is the owner or operator of a library bindery, when such is not the fact, or in any other manner to misrepresent the character, extent, volume, or type of his business.

(b) *Use of the Word "Free."* In connection with the sale, offering for sale, or distribution of industry products, it is an unfair trade practice to use the word "free," or any other word or words of similar import, in advertisements or in other offers to the public, as descriptive of an article of merchandise, or service, which is not an unconditional gift, under the following circumstances:

(1) When all the conditions, obligations, or other prerequisites to the receipt and retention of the "free" article of merchandise or service offered are not clearly and conspicuously set forth at the outset so as to leave no reasonable probability that the terms of the offer will be misunderstood; and, regardless of such disclosure:

(2) When, with respect to any article of merchandise required to be purchased in order to obtain the "free" article or service, the offerer (a) increases the ordinary and usual price of such article of merchandise, or (b) reduces its quality, or (c) reduces the quantity or size thereof.

(*Note:* The disclosure required by subsection b(1) of this rule shall appear in close conjunction with the word "free" (or other word or words of similar import) wherever such word first appears in each advertisement or offer. A disclosure in the form of a footnote, to which reference is made by use of an asterisk or other symbol placed next to the word "free," will not be regarded as compliance.)

(c) *Misbranding of Library Binding.* The false or deceptive marking, branding, or labeling of any library binding with respect to the grade, quality, use, effect, purpose, material, conformity to a trade standard, origin, preparation, manufacture, or conformity of such library binding, or concerning any component thereof, or in any other material respect, is an unfair trade practice.

RULE 2—GUARANTEES AND WARRANTIES.

(a) It is an unfair trade practice to use or cause to be used any guarantee or warranty which is false, misleading, deceptive, or unfair to the purchasers of library binding.

(b) Within the inhibitions of this rule is the use of the following types of guarantees:

(1) Guarantees containing statements, representations, or assertions which have the capacity and tendency or effect of misleading and deceiving in any material respect; or

(2) Guarantees which are of such form, text, or character as to import, imply, or represent that the guarantee is broader than is in fact true, or will afford more protection and service to purchasers or users than is in fact true; or

(3) Guarantees in which any condition, qualification, or contingency applied by the guarantor thereto is not fully and nondeceptively stated therein, or is stated in such manner or form as to be deceptively minimized, obscured, or concealed, wholly or in part; or

(4) Guarantees which are stated, phrased, or set forth in such

manner that although the statements contained therein are literally and technically true, the whole is misleading in that purchasers or users are not made sufficiently aware of certain contingencies or conditions applicable to such guarantees which materially lessen the value or protection thereof as guarantees to purchasers or users; or

(5) Guarantees which have the capacity and tendency or effect of otherwise misrepresenting the performance, serviceability, durability, or lasting qualities of library binding, such as, for example, a guarantee extending for a certain number of years or other long period of time when the ability of the library binding to last, endure, or remain serviceable for such period of time has not been established by actual experience or by competent and adequate tests definitely showing in either case that the library binding has such lasting qualities under the conditions encountered or to be encountered in the respective locality where the library binding is sold and used under the guarantee; or

(6) Guarantees under which the guarantor fails or refuses to observe scrupulously his obligations thereunder or fails or refuses to make good on claims coming reasonably within the terms of the guarantee; or

(7) Guarantees which are otherwise false, misleading, or deceptive.

(c) This rule shall be applicable not only to guarantees, but also to warranties, to purported warranties and guarantees, and to any promise or representation in the nature of or purporting to be a guarantee or warranty.

RULE 3—OTHER DECEPTION.

(a) *Deceptive Use and Imitation of Trade or Corporate Names, Trade-Marks, etc.* It is an unfair trade practice for any member of the industry—

(1) to imitate, or cause to be imitated, or directly or indirectly promote the imitation of, the trade-marks, trade names, or other exclusively owned symbols or marks of identification of competitors in a manner having the capacity and tendency or effect of misleading or deceiving purchasers, prospective purchasers, or the buying public; or

(2) to use any trade name, corporate name, trade-mark, or other trade designation which has the capacity and tendency or effect of misleading or deceiving purchasers or prospective purchasers as to the character, name, nature, or origin of any library bindery, or of any material used therein, or which is false or misleading in any other respect.

(b) *False or Deceptive Selling Methods.* To use or promote the use of any selling method or credit term which has the capacity and tendency or effect of misleading or deceiving the purchasing or consuming public is an unfair trade practice.

(c) *Substitution of Products.* The practice of shipping or delivering library binding which does not conform to specifications upon which the sale is consummated, or to representations made prior to securing the order, without the consent of the purchasers to such substitution, and with the capacity and tendency or effect of misleading or deceiving purchasers, is an unfair trade practice.

(d) *False Invoicing.* Withholding from or inserting in invoices any statement or information by reason of which omission or insertion a false record is made, wholly or in part, of the transactions represented on the face of such invoices, with the capacity and tendency or effect of thereby misleading or deceiving purchasers or prospective purchasers, is an unfair trade practice.

RULE 4—DECEPTIVE REPRESENTATIONS AS TO PRODUCTS CONFORMING TO A STANDARD OR SPECIFICATION.

In the sale, offering for sale, or distribution of any library binding, it is an unfair trade practice:

(a) To falsely represent or imply that any such library binding conforms to the requirements of any standard or specification, whether established or recognized by a department or unit of a city or state government, or of the Federal Government, by trade practice, or otherwise.

(b) To represent or imply that such library binding conforms to the requirements of any standard or specification without clearly disclosing the identity of the standard or specification to which reference is made. Such disclosure shall be by reference to the standard or specification on all labels, invoices, sales literature, and other advertising containing such representation or implication.

(c) For any member of the industry to claim or imply that the library binding conforms to any standard or specification which is inapplicable or which has been rescinded, revised, superseded, or amended, and thereby mislead or deceive purchasers or prospective purchasers.

RULE 5—FICTITIOUS PRICES, PRICE LISTS, ETC.

The publishing or circulating by any member of the industry of false or misleading price quotations, price lists, terms or conditions of sale, or false or misleading reports as to production or sales, with the capacity and tendency or effect of misleading or deceiving purchasers or prospective purchasers, or the advertising, sale, or offering for sale of library binding at prices purporting to be reduced from what are in fact fictitious prices, or at purported reductions in prices when such purported reductions are in fact fictitious or are otherwise misleading or deceptive, is an unfair trade practice.

RULE 6—SELLING BELOW COST.

The practice of selling industry products at a price less than the cost thereof to the seller, with the purpose or intent, and where the effect may be, to injure, suppress, or stifle competition or tend to create a monopoly in the production or sale of such products, is an unfair trade practice. As used in this rule, the term "cost" means the total cost to the seller, including the costs of acquisition, processing, preparation for marketing, sale, and delivery.

RULE 7—DEFAMATION OF COMPETITORS OR FALSE DISPARAGEMENT OF THEIR PRODUCTS.

The defamation of competitors by falsely imputing to them dishonorable conduct, inability to perform contracts, questionable credit standing, or by other false representations, or the false disparagement of the grade or quality of their library binding, or of their business methods, selling prices, values, credit terms, policies, services, or conditions of employment, is an unfair trade practice.

RULE 8—ENTICING AWAY EMPLOYEES OF COMPETITORS.

Knowingly enticing away employees or sales representatives of competitors under any circumstance having the capacity and tendency or effect of substantially injuring or lessening present or potential competition is an unfair trade practice; *provided,* that nothing in this rule shall be construed as prohibiting employees from seeking more favorable employment, or as prohibiting employers from hiring or offering employment to employees of competitors in good faith and not for the purpose of injuring, destroying, or preventing competition.

RULE 9—COMMERCIAL BRIBERY.

It is an unfair trade practice for a member of the industry, directly or indirectly, to give, or offer to give, or permit or cause to be given, money or anything of value to agents, employees, or representatives of customers or prospective customers, or to agents, employees, or representatives of competitors' customers or prospective customers, without the knowledge of their employers or principals, as an inducement to influence their employers or principals to purchase or contract to purchase products manufactured or sold by such industry member or the maker of such gift or offer, or to influence such employers or principals to refrain from dealing in the products of competitors or from dealing or contracting to deal with competitors.

RULE 10—PROCUREMENT OF COMPETITORS' CONFIDENTIAL INFORMATION.

It is an unfair trade practice for any member of the industry to obtain information concerning the business of a competitor by bribery of an employee or agent of such competitor, by false or misleading statements or representations, by the impersonation of one in authority, or by any other unfair means, and to use the information so obtained so as substantially to injure competition or unreasonably restrain trade.

RULE 11—UNLAWFUL INTERFERENCE WITH COMPETITORS' PURCHASES OR SALES.

It is an unfair trade practice for any industry member, by means of any monopolistic practices, or through combination, conspiracy, coercion, boycott, threats, or any other unlawful means, directly or indirectly to interfere with a competitor's right to purchase his raw materials and supplies from whomsoever he chooses, or to sell his product to whomsoever he chooses.

RULE 12—ARRANGEMENTS TO EXCLUDE SALE OF COM-PETITORS' PRODUCTS.

It is an unfair trade practice for any member of the industry to sell or contract for the sale of any industry products for use or resale, or to fix a price charged therefor, or discount from, or rebate upon, such price, on the condition, agreement, or understanding that the purchaser thereof shall not use or deal in new, used, or rebuilt products of a competitor or competitors of such industry member where the effect of such sale or contract for sale, or such condition, agreement, or under-standing, may be to substantially lessen competition or tend to create a monopoly in any line of commerce.

RULE 13—TIE-IN SALES—COERCING PURCHASE OF ONE PRODUCT AS A PREREQUISITE TO THE PURCHASE OF OTHER PRODUCTS.

The practice of coercing the purchase of one or more types of li-brary binding as a prerequisite to the purchase of one or more other types of library binding, where the effect may be substantially to lessen competition or tend to create a monopoly or unreasonably to restrain trade, is an unfair trade practice.

RULE 14—UNFAIR THREATS OF INFRINGEMENT SUITS.

The circulation of threats of suit for infringement of patents or trade-marks among customers or prospective customers of competitors, not made in good faith but for the purpose or with the effect of thereby harassing or intimidating such customers or prospective cus-tomers, or of unduly hampering, injuring, or prejudicing competitors in their business, is an unfair trade practice.

RULE 15—INDUCING BREACH OF CONTRACT.

Knowingly inducing or attempting to induce the breach of existing lawful contracts between competitors and their customers or their suppliers, or interfering with or obstructing the performance of any such contractual duties or services, under any circumstance having the capacity and tendency or effect of substantially injuring or lessening present or potential competition, is an unfair trade practice.

Nothing in this rule is intended to imply that it is improper for an industry member to solicit the business of a customer of a competing industry member; nor is the rule to be construed as in anywise author-izing any agreement, understanding, or planned common course of ac-tion by two or more industry members not to solicit business from the customers of either of them, or from customers of any other indus-try member.

RULE 16—PROHIBITED FORMS OF TRADE RESTRAINTS (UN-LAWFUL PRICE FIXING, ETC.).[1]

It is an unfair trade practice for any member of the industry, either directly or indirectly, to engage in any planned common course of ac-

---

[1] The inhibitions of this rule are subject to Public Law 542, approved July 14, 1952—66 Stat. 632 (the McGuire Act).

tion, or to enter into or take part in any understanding, agreement, combination, or conspiracy, with one or more members of the industry, or with any other person or persons, to fix or maintain the price of any goods or otherwise unlawfully to restrain trade; or to use any form of threat, intimidation, or coercion to induce any member of the industry or other person or persons to engage in any such planned common course of action, or to become a party to any such understanding, agreement, combination, or conspiracy.

RULE 17—PROHIBITED DISCRIMINATION.[2]

(a) *Prohibited Discriminatory Prices, or Rebates, Refunds, Discounts, Credits, Etc., Which Effect Unlawful Price Discrimination.* It is an unfair trade practice for any member of the industry engaged in commerce, in the course of such commerce, to grant or allow, secretly or openly, directly or indirectly, any rebate, refund, discount, credit, freight or other transportation cost or any percentage thereof, or other form of price differential, where such rebate, refund, discount, credit, freight or other transportation cost or any percentage thereof, or other form of price differential, effects a discrimination in price between different purchasers of goods of like grade and quality, where either or any of the purchases involved therein are in commerce, and where the effect thereof may be substantially to lessen competition or tend to create a monopoly in any line of commerce, or to injure, destroy, or prevent competition with any person who either grants or knowingly receives the benefit of such discrimination, or with customers of either of them: *Provided, however—*

(1) That the goods involved in any such transaction are sold for use, consumption, or resale within any place under the jurisdiction of the United States;

(2) That nothing herein contained shall prevent differentials which make only due allowance for differences in the cost of manufacture, sale, or delivery resulting from the differing methods or quantities in which such commodities are to such purchasers sold or delivered;

(3) That nothing herein contained shall prevent persons engaged in selling goods, wares, or merchandise in commerce from selecting their own customers in bona fide transactions and not in restraint of trade;

(4) That nothing herein contained shall prevent price changes from time to time where in response to changing conditions affecting the market for or the marketability of the goods concerned, such as but not limited to obsolescence of seasonal goods, distress sales un-

---

[2] As used in Rule 17, the word "commerce" means "trade or commerce among the several States and with foreign nations, or between the District of Columbia or any Territory of the United States and any State, Territory, or foreign nation, or between any insular possessions or other places under the jurisdiction of the United States, or between any such possession or place and any State or Territory of the United States or the District of Columbia or any foreign nation, or within the District of Columbia or any Territory or any insular possession or other place under the jurisdiction of the United States."

der court process, or sales in good faith in discontinuance of business in the goods concerned.

(b) *Prohibited Brokerage and Commissions.* It is an unfair trade practice for any member of the industry engaged in commerce, in the course of such commerce, to pay or grant, or to receive or accept, anything of value as a commission, brokerage, or other compensation, or any allowance or discount in lieu thereof, except for services rendered in connection with the sale or purchase of goods, wares, or merchandise, either to the other party to such transaction or to an agent, representative, or other intermediary therein where such intermediary is acting in fact for or in behalf, or is subject to the direct or indirect control, of any party to such transaction other than the person by whom such compensation is so granted or paid.

(c) *Prohibited Advertising or Promotional Allowances, Etc.* It is an unfair trade practice for any member of the industry engaged in commerce to pay or contract for the payment of advertising or promotional allowances or any other thing of value to or for the benefit of a customer of such member in the course of such commerce as compensation or in consideration for any services or facilities furnished by or through such customer in connection with the processing, handling, sale, or offering for sale of any products or commodities manufactured, sold, or offered for sale by such member, unless such payment or consideration is available on proportionally equal terms to all other customers competing in the distribution of such products or commodities.

(d) *Inducing or Receiving an Illegal Discrimination in Price.* It is an unfair trade practice for any member of the industry engaged in commerce, in the course of such commerce, knowingly to induce or receive a discrimination in price which is prohibited by the foregoing provisions of this Rule 17.

(e) *Prohibited Discriminatory Return and Exchange Privileges.* It is an unfair trade practice for any member of the industry to grant or contract to grant privileges of merchandise return, refund, exchange, or other special privileges, upon terms which, under the provisions of this Rule 17, effect any unlawful discrimination in price, services, or facilities in favor of one purchaser against another purchaser or purchasers.

(f) *Exemptions.* The inhibitions of this Rule 17 shall not apply to purchases of their supplies for their own use by schools, colleges, universities, public libraries, churches, hospitals, and charitable institutions not operated for profit.

(*Note:* In complaint proceedings charging discrimination in price or services or facilities furnished, and upon proof having been made of such discrimination, the burden of rebutting the prima facie case thus made by showing justification shall be upon the person charged; and unless justification shall be affirmatively shown, the Commission is authorized to issue an order terminating the discrimination: *Provided, however,* That nothing herein contained shall prevent a seller rebutting the prima facie case thus made by showing that his lower price or the furnishing of services or facilities to any purchaser or purchasers was made in good faith to meet an equally low price of a competitor, or the services or facilities furnished by a competitor. See Sec. 2(b) Clayton Act.)

RULE 18—AIDING OR ABETTING UNFAIR TRADE PRACTICES.

It is an unfair trade practice for any person, firm, or corporation to aid, abet, coerce, or induce another, directly or indirectly, to use or promote the use of any unfair trade practice specified in the foregoing rules.

Promulgated by the Federal Trade Commission August 20, 1954.

Robert M. Parrish,
Secretary.

APPENDIX 10

COSTS OF SERVICES WHICH MEET MINIMUM STANDARDS FOR PUBLIC LIBRARY SYSTEMS IN 1969

reprinted from
JUST BETWEEN OURSELVES, October 1969
Public Library Association
ALA: 50 East Huron Street, Chicago, Illinois 60611

In revising *Costs of Public Library Service* for 1969 the subcommittee has followed the same pattern as the previous year so that the various components of the budgets will be comparable. As before, sample budgets for library systems serving population groups of three different sizes have been prepared. These budgets are based on meeting the requirements of *Minimum Standards for Public Library Systems, 1966* and its *Statistical Standards* addenda.

Realizing that sample budgets must of necessity be somewhat arbitrary, the subcommittee believes that it would be helpful to list some of the factors which influence the preparation of actual budgets and which also cause wide variations in budgets for systems serving population groups of a similar size. The list is not meant to be exhaustive but does suggest some important considerations for budget planners.

MAJOR FACTORS WHICH INFLUENCE BUDGETS

A. The nature of the system

   1. The type of organizational structure
   2. The number of units to be
      a. staffed
      b. stocked with materials
      c. rented, depreciated, insured
      d. heated, lighted, cleaned, maintained
   3. The geographical area to be served
      a. size in square miles
      b. barriers such as mountains, rivers, limited-access highways, railroads, industrial complexes
      c. concentrations of population, whether centralized or scattered

B. Characteristics of the population to be served

   1. Rate of growth or decline
   2. Educational levels
   3. Socioeconomic status
   4. Employment opportunities available; level of unemployment—seasonal, cyclical, chronic

C. Staff

   1. Salary levels
      a. related to other positions in the area requiring similar training and experience
      b. adequate to attract qualified professional candidates nationally
      c. clerical salaries equivalent to those paid for similar work in the area
      d. adequate to attract non-library professionals, such as personnel officers, business managers, computer technicians, subject specialists, and the like
   2. Fringe benefits
      a. to cover ordinary illness and vacation needs of staff
      b. to assist in unusually prolonged illness or disability
      c. to enable staff to retire at a mandatory age set to benefit the employee, create promotional opportunities for younger staff, and maintain the efficiency of the system operation
      d. to encourage long tenure of staff exhibiting high potential for growth on the job
      e. to counterbalance necessary but unpopular hours and schedules
   3. Opportunities for professional growth
      a. in-system travel to book selection and other staff meetings
      b. continuing education: time with pay, tuition, and/or travel
      c. attendance at state, national, and other professional meetings

D. Age and quality of the existing materials collection; is it

   1. New, still being built up to reach the minimum per capita standards for all media?
   2. Meeting minimum standards, chiefly needing current additions and replacements?
   3. Inadequate in quality and depth; in need of weeding, extensive additions of basic titles, greater reference strength?
   4. Supplemented by nearby stronger, more specialized collections, access to which is financed by the state or by the system through contracts?
   5. Limited in variety by need to duplicate titles extensively because
      a. there are multiple outlets?
      b. central collections are departmentalized?

E. Operational services

   1. Those received from other governmental units without direct cost, such as purchasing, processing, bookkeeping, personnel recruiting and examining, maintenance, or utility franchises

2. Those for which costs must be included in the budget: contractual services such as the above, use of film circuit, interlibrary loan fees and postage, computer time, etc.

F. Costs of transportation
   1. Staff and library materials must be transported short distances only
   2. Staff must be transported long distances to insure face-to-face contacts between headquarters staff and unit staffs
   3. Library materials must be transported for long distances or in considerable quantities because
      a. borrowers may return materials to any branch or outlet
      b. units exchange substantial proportions of their collections
   4. Bookmobile purchase and maintenance

G. Need for experimental or innovative programs related to the social problems of a changing society

H. Planning and implementing long-range objectives for the system

THE SAMPLE BUDGETS

In preparing the budgets certain assumptions were made:

1. Each budget is a minimum for a total system with no distinction being made as to whether the system is consolidated or federated; nor has the subcommittee tried to separate local funds of member libraries from overall costs.
2. Each budget assumes optimum efficiency in administrative budgeting and coordinated planning among the units of the system.
3. Since there are no specific standards for library operating expenses other than for personnel and materials, it was assumed on the basis of experience and data found in previous cost supplements that these two categories would comprise approximately 85-90% of the total budget.

The subcommittee again wishes to emphasize that the budgets are illustrative only and do not represent those of any actual library systems.

The following comments will help to clarify the budgets and show how the various unit costs were obtained.

Personnel

The figure of $8,500 was established by the Board of Directors of the Public Library Association at its 1969 midwinter meeting in Washington as a reasonable beginning salary for a professional librarian for the current year.

Pay scales and classifications for professional positions follow those given in the *Statistical Standards* with positions added as necessary for the larger systems.

It is assumed that each hypothetical library system has carefully drawn job descriptions with personnel working at maximum efficiency.

The number of positions assigned at each professional grade level were necessarily based on subjective opinions, experience, and observation.

It was thought that the various professional grade levels would include professional personnel of other disciplines, such as business and personnel managers, publicity specialists, etc., as well as librarians.

Salaries of clerks and pages were determined by adding a percentage increase of approximately 12½% to the salaries established last year for these two categories. The federal minimum wage was used in 1968 as a beginning salary for pages, and clerical salaries computed accordingly.

Ten percent of the total personnel budget was allotted for benefits, i.e., pensions, insurance, hospitalization, etc. Vacation allowances were included in the regular salary budget. The subcommittee recognizes that there are many considerations which affect the salaries actually paid in various library systems and calls attention to those listed under "C" in *Major Factors Which Influence Budgets.*

Materials

The *Bowker Annual '69* gives $8.47[1] as the average cost of a book for the past year. Adding to this figure 6% for estimated price increase for 1969 and allowing a 20% average discount for *all* types of books purchased gives a unit cost of $7.18 per book or 14 cents more than in 1968.

The unit cost of $13.00 ($3.00 more than last year) allows for the inclusion of the specialized and scientific periodicals which library systems with comprehensive collections would be expected to own, while periodical titles commonly duplicated are figured at a unit cost of $12.00.

Unit costs of films and recordings were based on current prices. It was a subcommittee decision to allow 12-14% of the total materials budget for binding, rebinding, and microforms.

Other Operating Expense

This category includes the usual items of janitor service, utilities, rent, insurance, maintenance equipment, supplies, etc., plus allowances for travel, transportation, recruiting, continuing education for staff and trustees, and other unassigned expenditures.

As expected the cost of services to meet minimum standards for public library systems in 1969 has increased. The average cost *per capita* for the three hypothetical library systems is approximately $6.12 for the current year compared with $5.50 for 1968. The figures for each population group demonstrate, as in the previous year, that a system serving a large number of persons serves them at a lower cost *per capita* than a smaller system. Continuously rising salaries increase the proportion of the total budget spent for this category with a corresponding decrease in the percentage spent for materials. The table below indicates the percentage changes in the major budget categories for 1968 and 1969.

---

[1] Bowker Annual '71 gives $11.66 as average cost.

Population groups	200,000		600,000		1,000,000	
Budget percentages	1968	1969	1968	1969	1968	1969
Salaries	62	63	67	67	67	69
Materials	23	22	21	19	21	19
Other operating expense	15	15	12	14	12	12
	100	100	100	100	100	100
Cost per capita	$5.80	$6.43	$5.36	$6.03	$5.31	$5.91

Subcommittee on Revision of Costs of Public Library Services: 1969

Ruth Gregory
Public Library,
Waukegan, Illinois

Vivian Maddox
Public Library,
Milwaukee, Wisconsin

Eleanor Plain, Chairman
Public Library,
Aurora, Illinois

SPECIMEN BUDGET FOR A LIBRARY SYSTEM
SERVING A POPULATION OF 200,000

SALARIES

No. of Positions In Full-time Equivalents	Title	Beginning Salary	Actual Average Salary at Third Level of Five-Step Range	Totals
1	Director	$ 20,400	$ 22,491	$ 22,491
1	Asst. Director	18,700	20,117	20,117
2	Professional V	15,725	17,437	34,874
2	Professional IV	14,025	15,462	30,924
6	Professional III	11,900	13,120	78,720
8	Professional II	10,200	11,245	89,960
10	Professional I	8,500	9,371	93,710
4	Subprofessional	6,800	7,497	29,988
46	Clerical		5,700	262,200
20	Pages		3,600	72,000
100				
	Subtotal			$734,984
	Benefits (10% of subtotal)			73,498
	Salary total			$808,482

MATERIALS

Number	Type	Unit Cost	Totals
30,000	Books	$ 7.18	$ 215,400
800	Periodical titles	13.00	10,400
200	Periodical duplicates	12.00	2,400
100	Films, etc.	220.00	22,000
500	Sound recordings	5.00	2,500
	Binding, rebinding, microform (12%)		30,324
	Materials total		$ 283,024

OTHER OPERATING EXPENSE $ 192,615

BUDGET TOTALS

Salaries	$ 808,482	(63%)	
Materials	283,024	(22%)	
Other Operating Expense	192,615	(15%)	
Budget total	$1,284,121	(100%)	
COST PER CAPITA (200,000 people)	$6.42		

SPECIMEN BUDGET FOR A LIBRARY SYSTEM
SERVING A POPULATION OF 600,000

SALARIES

No. of Positions In Full-time Equivalents	Title	Beginning Salary	Actual Average Salary at Third Level of Five-Step Range	Totals
1	Director	$ 22,100	$ 24,365	$ 24,365
2	Asst. Director	20,400	22,491	44,982
3	Professional VI	18,700	20,117	60,351
5	Professional V	15,725	17,437	87,185
10	Professional IV	14,025	15,462	154,620
15	Professional III	11,900	13,120	196,800
24	Professional II	10,200	11,245	269,880
30	Professional I	8,500	9,371	281,130
10	Subprofessional	6,800	7,491	74,910
140	Clerical		5,700	798,000
60	Pages		3,600	216,000
300	Subtotal			2,208,223
	Benefits (10% of subtotal)			220,822
	Salary total			$2,429,045

MATERIALS

Number	Type	Unit Cost	Totals
75,000	Books	$ 7.18	$ 538,500
2,400	Periodical titles	13.00	31,200
600	Periodical duplicates	12.00	7,200
125	Films, etc.	220.00	27,500
1,500	Sound recordings	5.00	7,500
	Subtotal		611,900
	Binding, rebinding, microform (13% of subtotal)		79,547
	Materials total		$ 691,447

OTHER OPERATING EXPENSE $ 502,152

BUDGET TOTALS

Salaries	$2,429,045	(67%)
Materials	691,447	(19%)
Other Operating Expense	502,152	(14%)
Budget total	$3,622,644	(100%)

COST PER CAPITA (600,000 people) $6.03

SPECIMEN BUDGET FOR A LIBRARY SYSTEM SERVING A POPULATION OF 1,000,000

SALARIES

No. of Positions In Full-time Equivalents	Title	Beginning Salary	Actual Average Salary at Third Level of Five-Step Range	Totals
1	Director	$ 23,800	$ 26,240	$ 26,240
3	Asst. Director	22,100	24,365	73,095
2	Professional VII	20,400	22,491	44,982
2	Professional VI	18,700	20,117	40,234
4	Professional V	15,725	17,437	69,748
20	Professional IV	14,025	15,462	309,240
35	Professional III	11,900	13,120	459,200
35	Professional II	10,200	11,245	393,575
50	Professional I	8,500	9,371	468,550
15	Subprofessional	6,800	7,497	112,455
233	Clerical		5,700	1,328,100
100	Pages		3,600	360,000
	Subtotal			$3,685,419
	Benefits (10% of subtotal)			368,541
	Salary total			$4,053,960

MATERIALS

Number	Type	Unit Cost	Totals
125,000	Books	$ 7.18	$ 897,500
4,000	Periodical titles	13.00	52,000
1,200	Periodical duplicates	12.00	14,400
150	Films, etc.	220.00	33,000
2,000	Sound recordings	5.00	10,000
	Subtotal		1,006,900
	Binding, rebinding, microform (14% of subtotal)		140,966
	Materials total		$1,147,866

OTHER OPERATING EXPENSE $ 709,340

BUDGET TOTALS

Salaries	$4,053,960	(69%)
Materials	1,147,866	(19%)
Other Operating Expense	709,340	(12%)
Budget total	$5,911,166	(100%)
COST PER CAPITA (1,000,000 people)	$5.91	

APPENDIX 11

INSTRUCTIONS ON SALVAGING
WATER-DAMAGED BOOKS

(Prepared by Library Binding Institute)

Over the years, Library Binders have been called upon to salvage collections damaged by water. These may be the result of burst pipes, floods, or any similar catastrophe.

The salvaging of such damaged collections is the work of experts, but it can be done at a reasonable cost, provided the simple rules set out in this brochure are followed.

The most important thing to remember is that most libraries are not equipped to do this work themselves, and that the use of artificial means by untrained personnel can ruin collections that otherwise can be saved.

Certified Library Binders are skilled in the knowledge of restoring collections. They can and will assist you in every phase of the salvage operations.

These rules are very simple, require little use of important manpower, and should enable you to salvage most of your collection. Experience of Certified Library Binders in handling collections damaged by either floods or bursting pipes which have flooded libraries indicates that 90% of a collection can often be salvaged by following these simple rules.

These simple steps can save your library substantial sums of money, since properly rebound books will afford eighty-five, or more, circulations and can preserve a damaged collection almost intact. If you need any further information, please contact Library Binding Institute, 160 State Street, Boston, Massachusetts 02109.

FIVE RULES TO FOLLOW:

1. STAND THE BOOKS ON FORE-EDGE, WITH THE LEAVES FANNED OUT, IN A WARM ROOM WHERE THERE IS GOOD CIRCULATION, PREFERABLY WITH A FAN OR, FANS GOING. (THIS WILL TEND TO PREVENT MILDEW OR MOLD.)

2. DO NOT WIPE OFF MUD WHEN THE BOOK IS WET.

(IT IS NOT NECESSARY TO WIPE OFF THE MUD, SINCE
WHEN THE VOLUME IS REBOUND, THE COVER IS REMOVED
AND THE EDGES TRIMMED.)

3. DO NOT HEAT IN AN OVEN OR USE OTHER TYPES OF
ARTIFICIAL HEAT.

4. DO NOT TRY TO PRESS WET OR SWOLLEN VOLUMES.
(YOUR BINDER WILL EXPERTLY PUT THEM INTO PROPER
SHAPE.)

5. CONTACT YOUR CERTIFIED LIBRARY BINDER AS SOON
AS POSSIBLE.

Normally, volumes made with coated paper cannot be salvaged, but
other volumes, even though they have been wet through, the glue dis-
integrated in the spine, the covers muddy, and the volume dirty, swollen
and distorted, can be restored by rebinding, so that it is just as good
as new; indeed, probably better, since it will have a stronger construction after rebinding than before, if you specify that the rebinding be
according to the L.B.I. Standard for Library Binding "formerly the
Minimum Specifications of Class 'A' Binding of the Joint Committee
of American Library Association and Library Binding Institute."

One of the most important things to do is to call in your Certified
Binder early, since he will be able to give you expert help. You will
be surprised to see how beautiful and clean-looking your volumes will
be when they are returned to you.

APPENDIX 12

BIBLIOGRAPHY

Akademiia nauk USSR. *New methods for the restoration and preservation of documents and books.*

American Library Association. Library Technology Project. *Protecting the Library and Its Resources: A Guide to Physical Protection and Insurance.* Report on a study conducted by Gaeg-Babcock & Associates, Inc. Chicago, 1963. 322 p.

Banks, Paul N. "Paper cleaning" (New York) *Journal of the Guild of Book Workers,* 5: No. 1, Fall 1966, pp. 8-22.

Banks, Paul N. *Treating leather bookbindings.* Chicago, Newberry Library, November 1967. 4 p.

Barrow, William J. "Acidity: an undesirable property in paste and mending tissue." *American Archivist* 30, January 1967, pp. 190-3.

Barrow, William J. *Manuscripts and documents: their deterioration and restoration.* Charlottesville, Va., University of Virginia Press, 1955.

Cockerell, Douglas. *Bookbinding and the care of books.* London, Pitman, 1955. (5th ed.)

Cockerell, Sydney M. *The repairing of books.* London, Sheppard Press, 1958.

Csapodi, C. *Conservation of the manuscript and book collections at the Library of the Hungarian Academy of Sciences: methods and results, 1949-1964.* Budapest, 1965. (In English and Hungarian)

Cunha, G. D. M. *Conservation of library materials; a manual and bibliography on the care, repair, and restoration of library materials.* Scarecrow, 1967.

Cutter, C. "Restoration of paper documents and manuscripts." *College and Research Libraries* 28, November 1967, pp. 387-97.

"Florence" *Book Collector,* Spring 1967, v. 16, pp. 7-43 (Special issue).

Friedman, H. B. "Preservation of library materials, the state of the art." *Special Libraries* 59, October 1968, pp. 608-13.

Harrison, L. S. *Report on the deteriorating effects of modern light sources.* New York, Metropolitan Museum of Art, 1954.

Hensel, Evelyn and Peter D. Veillette. *Purchasing Library Materials in Public and School Libraries.* Chicago, American Library Association and the National League of Cities, 1969.

Horton, Carolyn. *Cleaning and preserving bindings and related materials.* Chicago, American Library Association, 1967. (Library Technology Program Publication No. 12) Second Edition, Revised, 1969 (Library Technology Project Publication No. 16).

Innes, R. F. "The preservation of vegetable-tanned leather against deterioration." *Progress in Leather Science,* chapter 18. London, British Leather Manufacturers' Research Association, 1948, pp. 426-50.

Kozulina, O. V., ed. *The hygiene and restoration of books in the city library.* Moscow, V. I. Lenin Library, 1960.

Langwell, W. H. *The conservation of books and documents.* London: Pitman, 1957.

Library Quarterly, January, 1970, issue.

Lodevijks, X. J. "The influences of light on museum objects." *Recent advances in conservation.* ed. by G. Thomson. London, Butterworths, 1963, pp. 7-8.

Lydenberg, Harry M., and Archer, John. *The care and repair of books.* 4th rev. ed. New York, Bowker, 1960.

Minogue, A. E. "The repair and preservation of records." *Bulletin of the National Archives, #5,* 1943.

Nordstrand, O. K. "Chinese double-leaved books and their restoration." *Libri* 17, no. 2, 1967, pp. 104-30.

Plenderleith, H. J. *The conservation of antiquities and works of art, treatment, repair, and restoration.* London, Oxford University Press, 1956.

Plenderleith, H. J. *The preservation of leather bookbindings.* London, British Museum, 1947.

Plumba, W. J. *The preservation of books in tropical and sub-tropical countries.* Kuala Lumpur, Oxford University Press, 1964.

Poole, F. G. "Preservation costs and standards." *Special Libraries* 59, October 1968, pp. 614-19.

"Preservation: the necessary art." *Fortune,* vol. 75, No. 3, March 1967, pp. 159-62.

Restaurator; an international journal for the preservation of library and archival material; v. 1, no. 1, 1969-   . Copenhagen, Restaurator press, 1969-.

Roberts, M. T. "Oversewing and the problem of book preservation in the research library." *College and Research Libraries* 28, January 1967, pp. 17-24.

Santucci, Ludovico. "The application of chemical and physical methods to conservation of archival materials." *Recent advances in conservation,* ed. by G. Thomson. London, Butterworths, 1963, pp. 39-47.

Shaffer, Norman J. "Library of Congress pilot preservation project." *College and Research Libraries* 30, January 1969, pp. 5-11.

Smith, R. D. "Paper impermanence as a consequence of pH and storage conditions." *Library Quarterly* 39: 153-95, April, 1969.

Storm, Colton. "Care, maintenance and restoration." *Rare book collections,* ed. by H. Richard Archer. Chicago, ACRL Monograph No. 27, American Library Association, 1965.

Tauber, Maurice F., *et al., Technical services in libraries,* New York, Columbia University Press, 1954.

Tauber, Maurice F., and Feinberg, Hilda (eds.). *Book catalogs.* Metuchen, N.J., Scarecrow Press, 1971.

Tribolet, Harold W. "Trends in preservation." *Library Trends* 13: no. 2, 1964, pp. 208-214.

UNESCO. *Conservation of cultural property with special reference to tropical conditions.* Paris, Unesco, 1968.

Vaccaro, E. "Vita e attivita istituzionale dell' Istituto di patologia del libro Alfonso Gallo." (Institutional life and activity of the Alfonso

Gallo Institute of Book Pathology.) *Accademie e Biblioteche d'Italia* 35, November 1967, pp. 462-7.

Von Dobeneck, Marianne. *A guide to binding practices and procedures.* 4th rev. ed., July, 1969. New York, Columbia University Libraries, Binding Department, 1969.

Waters, Peter. "Book restoration after the Florence floods." *Penrose Annual* 62, 1969, Hastings House, pp. 83-93.

Weidner, Marilyn Kemp. "Damage and deterioration of art on paper due to ignorance and the use of faulty materials." *Studies in Conservation* 12: pp. 5-25, 1967.

Williams, Gordon R. "The preservation of deteriorating books," Part I: An examination of the problem," *Library Journal* 91, January 1, 1966, pp. 51-56; Part II: Recommendations for a solution," January 15, 1966, pp.189-193.

Zaehnsdorf, Joseph W. *The art of bookbinding: A practical treatise.* 8th ed. London, Bell, 1914.

Zigrosser, Carl and Christa M. Gaehde. *A guide to the collecting and care of original prints.* New York, Crown, 1965 (sponsored by The Print Council of America).

APPENDIX 13

FEDERAL FUNDS FOR YOUR
SCHOOL AND LIBRARY

The Federal government began a program of aid to education in the 1960's which included financial assistance to libraries. These programs are scattered over several hundred statutes and administered by several agencies. For library purposes, the principal agency is the Department of Health, Education and Welfare.

Programs are administered in various ways: Some directly from Washington, others through state library or school library departments.

The following chart indicates programs in effect in 1969. For current information, consult the Department of Health, Education and Welfare.

ELEMENTARY & SECONDARY EDUCATION ACT OF 1965:

TITLES	MATCHING FUNDS	HOW ADMINISTERED	U. S. GOVERNMENT AGENCY	ELIGIBLE RECIPIENTS	ELIGIBLE EXPENDITURES
TITLE I—Assistance to local educational agencies where there are high concentrations of children from low-income families (As amended)	Yes—Formula in Statute	State Education Agency	U. S. Dept. of Health, Education & Welfare Office of Education Div. of Program Operations	School District (including pre-school programs)	Purchase of books, prebinds, paperbacks, bound periodicals and rebinding of books and periodicals.
TITLE II—Federal grants to public schools and loans of materials to children and teachers in private schools	No	State Education Agency	U. S. Dept. H.E.W. Office of Education Div. of Plans & Supplementary Centers	Public Schools and loans to children and teachers in private schools	School resources, textbooks and instructional materials. Includes books, prebound books, prebound periodicals. books and periodicals purchased and sent to a binder to be library bound (before delivery to the school). Excluded by Regulation are repair, redistribution and rebinding.
TITLE III—Grants to supplementary educational centers to upgrade the quality of education	Federal Funds supplement local funds	U. S. H.E.W. Commissioner of Education & Advisory Council	See above	Applicants: Local educational agencies	Project may provide for expenditures for acquisition of books and periodicals and rebinding.
TITLE V—Grants to strengthen state departments of education	None prior to July 1, 1967	State Education Agency	U. S. Dept. H.E.W. Office of Education	State Educational Agency (State and NOT local level)	Binding of books and periodicals may be included in state plan. NOTE: TITLE VI defines equipment to mean printed, published, audiovisual, books, periodicals, documents and related materials.

TITLES	MATCHING FUNDS	HOW ADMINISTERED	U. S. GOVERNMENT AGENCY	ELIGIBLE RECIPIENTS	ELIGIBLE EXPENDITURES
NATIONAL DEFENSE EDUCATION ACT As Amended by P.L. 88-665: TITLE III—Financial assistance to strengthen instruction in specific subjects SEE ALSO: Similar to TITLE III is Section 12 of Act to Establish National Foundation of the Arts & Humanities and TITLE VI of Higher Education Act of 1965 pertaining to undergraduate college education.	Yes	State Education Agency	U. S. Dept. H.E.W. Office of Education	Schools and junior colleges part of a secondary system and audiovisual libraries part of a local educational system	Purchase of materials to strengthen instruction in science, mathematics, modern foreign languages, English, history, civics, geography and economics, including books (prebinds and paperbacks), reference books and periodicals. Excluded are textbooks and any processing.
TITLE I—PUBLIC LIBRARY SERVICES See also: Section 214, Appalachian Regional Development Act of 1965	Federal funds match state and local expenditures	State Library Agency program subject to Federal approval of State Plan	U. S. Dept. H.E.W. Office of Education Division of Library Services & Educational Facilities Library Services Branch	Urban and rural areas which lack public libraries or have inadequate services	A plan may include expenditures for books, periodicals and binding
HIGHER EDUCATION ACT OF 1965 (AS AMENDED) TITLE I—COMMUNITY SERVICE & CONTINUING EDUCATION PROGRAMS	Federal funds supplement state funds	Existing or new state agency	U. S. Dept. H.E.W. Office of Education Bureau of Adult & Vocational Education (Div. of Adult Education) (Commissioner advised by National Advisory Council on Extension and Continuing Education)	State or participating institutions—or both	All expenditures in approved plan for new, expanded or improved community programs

TITLES	MATCHING FUNDS	HOW ADMINISTERED	U. S. GOVERNMENT AGENCY	ELIGIBLE RECIPIENTS	ELIGIBLE EXPENDITURES
TITLE II—COLLEGE LIBRARY ASSISTANCE AND LIBRARY TRAINING & RESEARCH PART A—College Library Resources	Applicant must spend an amount equal to average annual amount it spent for eligible materials during two-year period ending June 30, 1965	Commissioner of Education, Washington, D. C.	U. S. Dept. H.E.W. Office of Education Library Services & Educational Facilities Division	Institutions of Higher Education—Three types of grants: Basic (maximum of $5,000 to each recipient) Supplemental (not in excess of $10 for each full-time student and equivalent of part-time students Special grants	Books, periodicals, documents, magnetic tapes, phonograph records, audiovisual materials and other related library materials (including necessary binding) Title II, Part A, Section 201
HIGHER EDUCATION ACT OF 1965 (AS AMENDED) TITLE II—COLLEGE LIBRARY ASSISTANCE AND LIBRARY TRAINING & RESEARCH PART B—Library Training & Research	None	Grants to institutions of higher education	U. S. Dept. H.E.W. Office of Education Bureau of Research	Grants for research and demonstration projects, including development of new techniques, systems and equipment for processing, storing and distributing information and dissemination of information derived from such research and demonstration	Expenditures as provided in grant
TITLE II—COLLEGE LIBRARY ASSISTANCE AND LIBRARY TRAINING & RESEARCH PART C—Strengthening College & Research Library Resources	None	Transfer of funds from Commissioner of Education to Librarian of Congress	U. S. Dept. H.E.W. Office of Education Bureau of Higher Education	Librarian of Congress	All library materials currently published throughout the world which are of value to scholarship and to provide and distribute catalog and bibliographic materials (materials may be purchased and bound where necessary)

TITLES	MATCHING FUNDS	HOW ADMINISTERED	U. S. GOVERNMENT AGENCY	ELIGIBLE RECIPIENTS	ELIGIBLE EXPENDITURES
TITLE III—STRENGTHENING DEVELOPING INSTITUTIONS	To increase and not to supplant existing funds	Grants to institutions	U. S. Dept. H.E.W. Office of Education (With Advisory Council on Developing Institutions)	"Developing Institutions", as defined in Section 302 and other cooperating institutions	Joint use of facilities such as libraries or laboratories, including necessary books, materials and equipment
TITLE VI—FINANCIAL ASSISTANCE FOR THE IMPROVEMENT OF UNDERGRADUATE INSTRUCTION PART A—Equipment	Federal funds shall not exceed 50% (or 80% where institution has insufficient resources) of expenditures	Existing or new state agency, state plan	U. S. Dept. H.E.W. Office of Education Associate Commissioner Bureau of Higher Education	Institutions of higher education	Laboratory and other equipment, including audiovisual and printed materials suitable for use in undergraduate instruction (except textbooks)

INDEX